# SEX AND
# THE CONFESSIONAL

# SEX AND THE CONFESSIONAL

NORBERTO VALENTINI
CLARA DI MEGLIO

TRANSLATED BY *Melton S. Davis*

STEIN AND DAY/*Publishers*/New York

# CONTENTS

6 *Contents*

# FOREWORD

WHEN IN 1964 a French magazine published an article which included five or six confessions taken down in shorthand unknown to the priests of several Paris churches, it set off a huge scandal. The magazine received over four thousand letters of protest, filled with invective and threats. Church authorities accused the editor of having violated the most important and intimate Christian sacrament, the one that provides redemption, and of doing it with indecent premeditation.

On that occasion, I wrote in *Monde Moderne*, the magazine of the International Institute of Sociology in Paris, the following: "Confession is an intimate and private dialogue between penitent and priest, but it's between *that* penitent and *that* priest. When it is depersonalized, it becomes a useful reference in examining the relationship between the synthesis of Christianity expressed by the priest and the external environment expressed by the penitent. As such, it is a most important subject for psychological and sociological research."

When I wrote this, I, too, found myself involved in a heated and unpleasant dispute. The official church objected that the return to grace is the eminent result of God's mercy and because of this there is no room for psychology or sociology.

7

After several months, however, those shorthand texts began to appear in authoritative religious magazines. They were accompanied by remarks and comments of various kinds, most of which were psychological in nature and therefore difficult to ignore in this age.

I suggested: "Why should we stop at the discussion of five or six confessions which, among other things, are not even indicative? Why not extend this research and use scientific methodology?"

What followed was another chorus of protests, and very little was done to follow my suggestions. Very little, that is, until now.

Included in this daring book are portions of more than six hundred confessions, collected on tape and based on characteristic situations carefully worked out beforehand. Because the priest in each case knew nothing of these preparations, the arguments used by him are all authentic. The material has been gathered from all parts of Italy.

This book, despite its limitation of concentrating on sexual sins (possibly to keep it within understandable bounds but leaving it open to protest from instant moralists), offers sociologists like myself a valuable source for surveys of wide human interests. For the church, it should serve as a stimulus for objective meditation.

I would not like to be in the shoes of the authors. They will meet with severe charges and cruel but unjustified moral lynchings. Because I know that they are fully aware of the dangers, my admiration for them is even greater. I am also convinced that this work will eventually be widely appreciated by all, especially by those who at first will be distressed by it.

Professor Pierre Dondaine
*Director of the International*
*Institute of Sociology, Paris*

# SEX AND
# THE CONFESSIONAL

# INTRODUCTION

## MODERN MAN AND CONFESSION

THE SCIENTIFIC revolution has radically changed society and caused a deep crisis in the relationship between the official Catholic Church and the individual. This crisis has worsened because of the widening gap in comprehension between the language of theology and the reality of everyday life.

Catholic dogmatism is based on an absolute truth. Scientific knowledge, on the other hand, is always relative and susceptible to modification. Contemporary man, being affected by explosive scientific developments, has more and more difficulty in believing in absolutes and in any dogma that requires strict obedience. He has begun to believe that morality is a collection of values that are variable and adaptable to environment and culture.

The split between the Church and the individual is demonstrated by the shocking statistics of worldwide absenteeism. In Italy, for instance, out of every hundred registered Catholics, only thirty attend mass on Sundays. Out of those thirty, only four confess periodically and receive Communion. And this statistic comes from one of the most Catholic countries.

The phenomenon is due to a combination of factors, two of

11

which are the most germane. The first is that the modern individual feels an instinctive intolerance toward the priest's archaic way of speaking, which is often awkward and based on rites and references which belong to another century. Worse yet is that much of what local priests say is even theologically wrong.

The second factor is that the priest often is not able to understand the problems of his flock, immersed as they are in a reality from which he is estranged.

Starting from these premises, we felt it important to carry out a survey of one of the obligatory and much-discussed paths followed in the priest-flock relationship—confession. Statistics from a Catholic source in 1939 showed that 46 per cent of Catholics confessed at least once a month and 67 per cent fulfilled their Easter duties. The fact that in the seventies only 4 per cent confess at least once a month and only 18 per cent fulfill their Easter duties is conclusive proof of the unease felt between the priest and modern man. With a view to overcoming this unease, certain theologians, headed by the Hungarian abbot Zoltan Alszeghy, have proposed radical reform of the sacrament of penance. The central tenet of this reform is joint confession, which takes place during the first part of the mass.

The documentation we give in the following pages represents something new in the history of the Church: heretofore unpublished material, recorded on tape at the source—that is, in the confessional.

Upon what bases, and in what spirit, are the conversations of the confessional carried out in the seventies? What are the reasons for incomprehension, the breach between penitent and priest? Has there been any change in the concept of sin? We are trying to answer these and other questions by means of this survey. We also hope to provide those who are studying this problem with material that is ample and, above all, authentic.

## WHY SEXUAL CONFESSIONS?

According to Father Roland Keynes, an expert in sexual morality, "One of the main reasons, if not the principal one, for the present crisis in the penitential sacrament is that it is becoming increasingly difficult for a Christian to understand which rulings on sexuality are valid and which are not." On the other hand, a 1966 survey in France indicates that 83 per cent of the sins confessed to the priest are of a sexual nature.

Sex influences all relations between two persons. Without arriving at a philosophy of *sexistentialism*—according to which sex is the only possible way to give significance to existence—it seems obvious that in every human action a definite sexual component does exist. Sexuality, therefore, is one of the factors that affects the balance, harmony, and capacity for development of the human personality.

For this reason, wanting to carry out research on confession and not being able to extend it to the infinite manifestations of sin (a seventeenth-century pamphlet lists 2753 ways of sinning), we have limited the survey to sex questions, taking into consideration the causes of the rift between Christian conscience and social reality.

The Church has always associated sex and sexuality with the concept of shame and guilt. Surely the time has passed when seminary students referred to the male organ as the "diabolical serpent" and the vagina as "Satan's den." In those days, mirrors were forbidden in baths, and a substance known as "modesty powder" was scattered in the bath water to cloud its transparency. Times have changed, but the priest, alas, continues to carry with him the heritage of past centuries. He finds himself unprepared in the face of modern man's very real problems.

Psychology and anthropology have partially rescued man from religious taboos. This change, however, brings with it new and disquieting problems. What standards does he use to establish his decisions? Do universal, unchanging norms exist, or are they conditioned by historical and cultural periods?

The trend in modern society is toward the removal of laws concerning sex. This fact engages people in a quest for a set of guidelines which will permit them to integrate their sexual activity into the complex of their personality.

But how does the Church react? Does it try to adapt itself or does it continue to hold out behind its historic barricade?

It would be easy to reply that the Church tries to adapt itself and to quote some of the more liberal thinkers in the Catholic theological circles. But one should not deceive oneself. These are the opinions of an elite which is isolated and almost always opposed by the official hierarchy.

What, on the other hand, is the stand taken by the main body of the Church? It is just this question that we are trying to answer with our survey.

## TAPE RECORDING IN THE CONFESSIONAL

Our survey has an essential value. It shows us, from the inside, what confession really is through a new and authentic documentation: the gathering, by means of a tape recorder, of 636 conversations actually held within the confessional.

How was this possible? Once we had decided to carry out the survey, we found ourselves faced with the problem of obtaining recorded material (material that remains and is thus absolutely valid). Obviously it would not be proper to *steal*, or listen to, other people's confessions, from either an ethical or a legal point of view. Therefore, we engaged in some preliminary research—going through pages of statistics and having private consultations with priests. The result of this research was a list of the most frequently confessed sexual sins which have broad social import. These included sexual relations prior to marriage, love play in conjugal relationships, birth-control practices, extramarital relationships of separated partners, and masturbation.

Having obtained this framework, we worked out some characteristic situations. With these, we then traveled throughout Italy, putting them forward directly in 636 confessionals. And we recorded these conversations, word by word, pause by pause, exclamation by exclamation. In 477 of the recordings made, the penitent addressing the priest is a woman; in 159 it is a man. In this way we have respected statistics that indicate that three out of every four who go to confession are women. Later, contrary to our expectations, we noted that the stand taken by the priest does not make much difference between a confession of a man or woman penitent.

The material collected was then selected and subdivided into the six categories that make up the following chapters. The first category reflects the situation of married couples faced with the problem of keeping their mutual physical attraction alive—that is, does the Church permit them to indulge in "love play"? The second concerns the situation of betrothed couples who have never engaged in intercourse but would like to do so. The third again concerns engaged couples, those who have already had intercourse and who ask the priest if they can continue without having to feel excluded from the Church. The fourth concerns unmarried women, no longer young, who have to grapple with problems of sex and love without a suitable matrimonial partner. The fifth concerns the reconciling of married partners' sexual needs with a wish to limit the number of children. The last concerns people who are separated from their spouses but who wish to begin a new love life.

The most indicative conversations are reported in full, omitting those in which there is duplication. We have also restricted comment to a minimum, feeling that the conversations themselves offer sufficient material for serious and useful reflection.

# I

## *LIMITS TO PERMISSIBLE LOVE PLAY*

St. Paul in his letter to the Corinthians said in reponse to questions about marriage that "it would be better for man not to touch woman," but that it would also be "better to marry than to burn."

Although this controversial sentence in the Bible has had many interpretations, it has been used to reinforce the Catholic Church's attitude that marriage is not a blessing but the lesser of evils. Intended or not, such a message gives the impression to some that everything connected with sex is an expression of sin.

Psychologists have shown that sex is not a sin but a demonstration of love, a quest for real communication. They have drawn attention to its human importance, noting that refraining from the sex act may cause quarrels, misunderstandings, infidelity, separation, and divorce.

The world, then, has begun to reject a morality which said that a person should "make children but not make love," a rule which meant that the biological duty was performed as quickly as possible in the dark "so that the guardian angel would not blush with shame." But what about the Church?

In this first series of conversations, the priests were asked what is permitted and what is not in demonstrations preparatory to the sexual act in a Christian marriage. Ninety-six conversations were recorded live in the confessionals. The results were nearly unanimous: in marriage everything is allowed (in some cases the priest even justifies some deviations), just as long as the final act is concluded completely.

## AS A PREPARATION FOR NORMAL INTERCOURSE

We give below the most indicative tape-recorded conversations among the ninety-six that concerned this type of situation.

### CHURCH OF SANT 'AGOSTINO, MONTEPULCIANO

PRIEST: How long is it since you confessed?

PENITENT: About three or four months.

PRIEST: What sins have you committed?

PENITENT: I don't know, but lately I sense my husband has lost interest in me. Maybe it's because I'm a bit too reluctant in marital relations. I'd like to know what I can do about it.

PRIEST: Have you given your husband any reason, personally, to provoke this?

PENITENT: No, no. I'm rather shy and perhaps I ought to take the initiative and do certain things. Is it allowed, in the Church, to do these things?

PRIEST: Yes, especially when it's a case of saving a marriage. The least that you can do is to desire the marital relationship. Be more affectionate, more expansive at certain moments. Have you every refused your conjugal obligations?

PENITENT: No, no, but the fact is that at the beginning I may have hesitated, and then I was ashamed. But now it seems to me that I must respond more, mustn't I?

PRIEST: Definitely. I believe that there is nothing more frustrating for a man than feeling that the woman is not participating. So, even if you—

PENITENT: No, I like it too. But I have a feeling of modesty that—

PRIEST: I see. But this feeling of modesty need not necessarily displease your husband. It's just that you ought to participate in the conjugal act. It's not that you must ask him to carry out these duties all by himself.

PENITENT: But that's just it. it's been quite some time since he . . .

PRIEST: Yes?

PENITENT: Well, I'd like to take the initiative and—

PRIEST: Look, you must make an effort, not just at the moment, but throughout the whole day. Do you understand, madam? You must be more tranquil. Even if at certain times you're nervous, you must not let anyone see it. How long have you been married?

PENITENT: Six years.

PRIEST: Six years. Have there been other times when nothing happened?

PENITENT: I'm afraid he's found another woman, you see.

PRIEST: Well, you'll be able to discover that if this absence, this coldness on his part, continues. You must not make jealous scenes.

PENITENT: No, no, not that. But I want . . . I want to know whether I can. . .

PRIEST: Try to arouse his interest?

PENITENT: Yes, but then can I . . . can I do all the—

PRIEST: You, for instance, must be careful in your dress, even in the house. Pay attention to your appearance. Try to be elegant, desirable too, otherwise something is lost and he's led to look elsewhere. These small things, as well as physical acts, have a great effect on men.

PENITENT: Look, I want to know whether, when we're in bed, I can snuggle up to him, I mean if I can try to—

PRIEST: Certainly.

PENITENT: But if I take the initiative, isn't it a sin?

PRIEST: No! Whoever said it was? As the man can take the initiative, madam, so can the woman. This physical need is the same for man as for woman. There is no reason why you shouldn't ask for it, provoke it.

PENITENT: Some time ago, I refused to enter into some love play because it seemed to me to be . . . er . . . immoral.

PRIEST: One must distinguish. You see, they're valid, they're permissible for the Church only in connection with the conjugal act. Even using the mouth, the eyes, any part of you, just as long as the conjugal act is the final objective. You ought not to do it if you were to think that with this physical preparation for the conjugal act . . . if you were to be quite sure, I mean, that the conjugal act would then be interrupted. Do you understand?

PENITENT: All right, this is an aspect—

PRIEST: Yes, just as long as it it your intention to complete the conjugal act.

PENITENT: Even if I like it? I mean, I won't be committing a sin? It's not that I just have to do as my husband wants and that's all?

PRIEST: No, no, no. You have just as much right to physical pleasure as he has. That's a mistake a lot of women make!

PENITENT: Yes, but a priest once told me that I could submit to everything my husband did just as long as I had no responsibility, in the sense that I didn't feel any pleasure.

PRIEST: But that's stupidity. You have equal rights. It's permissible, within marriage, to satisfy one's senses. This has probably held you back from participating actively in the marital act. But, like your husband, you have every right to physical satisfaction. And to arrive at the conjugal act, you may also prepare for it. Have you any children?

PENITENT: Yes, two.

PRIEST: Two children. There you are. You see, your way of thinking about these things is outdated.

PENITENT: But who says that it's an outdated way of thinking? The Church, for instance, only a few years ago—

PRIEST: It's not that the Church has changed. It's just that at a certain point it had to say these things.

PENITENT: Yes, all right, but once, for instance, when we were engaged, the parish priest said that we couldn't even kiss each other because it was a sin.

PRIEST: That, too, is stupidity.

PENITENT: I don't understand.

PRIEST: It's not that the Church's doctrine has changed.

PENITENT: Yes, but there was a time when I abided by these things you call stupidities—that kissing was a sin and so on—because I was taught them in church. But now, instead, they become—

PRIEST: But it's always been so, there are books that say so.

PENITENT: Why, then, did you priests tell us these things?

PRIEST: Look, ever since I've been a priest, I've always told my young people this. I've told them these things plainly. Unfortunately, ignorance has made many people unhappy. So, you may go with your conscience at peace. You have a right to physical pleasure just like your husband. And with a view to the conjugal act you may seek, you may prepare. I'll say even more. They probably told you many times that the thought of having a physical contact with your husband is a sin. That's not true at all. If you think about this act with your husband with a view to the conjugal act which within marriage is permissible, it is not a bad thought. For heaven's sake! So you, being in bed with your husband, do not necessarily have to accept him passively although desiring him. After all, who says that a woman doesn't desire the conjugal act just as the man does? At certain times she desires it much more than a man, because her sensations are much more profound than a man's. She must not just remain passive and merely consent to what the husband wants, indeed she may manifest her desire with a clear conscience, through acts, caresses.

PENITENT: All right.

PRIEST: You mustn't feel any fear. The important thing is that your intention be that of defending the conjugal union and of having conjugal relations such as are permitted in marriage, when you want to and how you want to. So you can feel completely serene with a clear conscience, do you understand?

PENITENT: Yes.

PRIEST: And, among other things, if you play the leading part in this relationship, you can find out also whether, by any chance, something else has come into your husband's life. Do you understand?

PENITENT: All right.

PRIEST: So don't worry. Keep calm, pray to Our Lord to help in solving this problem. For penance, say three Hail Marys to Our Lady.


CHURCH OF SAN LORENZO, NAPLES

PRIEST: How long is it since you confessed?

PENITENT: It's been about two years, I'm not sure, maybe more.

PRIEST: How's that? Is there any special reason?

PENITENT: Well, yes, Father. You see, I'm married and I have a sexual relationship with my husband that my confessor at that time didn't approve of. But now, I've been reading a little book, approved by the ecclesiastic authorities, which says that love play in marriage is allowed and, in fact, that it gives substance to marriage. And so I thought that I wasn't outside the Church, as I believed I was.

PRIEST: How long have you been married?

PENITENT: Five years.

PRIEST: And how old are you?

PENITENT: Twenty-eight. Why?

PRIEST: Look, love play isn't forbidden . . . but why do you call it love play? They are acts which excite, which lead up to coitus, aren't they?

PENITENT: Oh, well, the little book called them that.

PRIEST: Listen, why have you chosen me as your confessor?

PENITENT: This is the church nearest to where I live.

PRIEST: Do you have faith in me as a confessor?

PENITENT: I don't know, I think so. Why?

PRIEST: Because we have to talk about this, and it's not an easy thing, you know. You must explain to me a bit to make it possible for me to understand.

PENITENT: Understand what?

PRIEST: What are the acts, the love play, that you engage in with your husband, do you understand? [*Long pause*] There are acts and acts, do you see?

PENITENT: Well, things to excite us, Father, nothing more. I don't think it's necessary to go into details.

PRIEST: I suppose that you strip naked and allow yourself to be . . . I mean, he looks at you and caresses you?

PENITENT: Well, yes. It's natural, isn't it?

PRIEST: Sure, sure. God gave you a body for this also. [*Pause*] And kisses? Does he kiss you?

PENITENT: Why, yes, Father. But is this really necessary? I mean, I feel a bit embarrassed talking about things like this.

PRIEST: You mustn't feel embarrassment, my child. Would you be embarrassed at the doctor's? The confessor is the doctor of your soul. How can I tell you what things are sinful if I don't know how you behave? Do you see?

PENITENT: All right.

PRIEST: Well, then, kisses?

PENITENT: Yes, of course.

PRIEST: Affectionate or lascivious?

PENITENT: I don't know, we do the things we do because we love each other.

PRIEST: What I mean is, kisses on the mouth or all over the body, on the breast, between the legs?

PENITENT: Yes.

PRIEST: You see, this may be sin, my child, or it may not be. It depends what you expect to get from this excitement. If they serve to get you in a condition ... and then he enters into you with his organ and you are joined in a Christian manner, it's not a sin. Otherwise it is, do you see?

PENITENT: But we scarcely ever perform the complete act, I mean, as you understand it. We don't want too many children. Anyway, it seems to me that the Church has admitted recently that the sexual act doesn't have to be exclusively for procreation. It can be a pleasurable act just for its own sake, isn't that so?

PRIEST: Partly, yes. And do you kiss him?

PENITENT: Yes.

PRIEST: His sexual organ as well? And do you give him pleasure?

PENITENT: But—

PRIEST: I've told you that you need not be ashamed. If you feel shame when talking with your confessor, it means that you think you're doing wrong and if you yourself think you're doing wrong, it's a sin.

PENITENT: It's not shame, it's embarrassment. You priests are the ones who have inculcated in us the idea that everything to do with sex is sinful. For centuries.

PRIEST: But times have changed. You see, my child, how I am speaking to you with extreme frankness. So?

PENITENT: All right, yes.

PRIEST: This you may do, my child, but when he is about to have pleasure, you must offer him your womb, because the act must end in there.

PENITENT: Yes, but we can't do that. I've already told you why.

PRIEST: My child, God doesn't wish that the seed be wasted, you understand? It's a sin to disperse the seed ... The sexual act is a material act that becomes ennobled solely by the knowledge that a new life may be born of it.

PENITENT: I thought it was ennobled by love.

PRIEST: Also.

PENITENT: I don't see anything noble about bringing children into the world and then finding it difficult to feed and educate them.

PRIEST: All you have to do is to be careful on the days the woman is fertile. As you know, my child, a woman is fertile only three or four days in the month.

PENITENT: But you can never feel sure!

PRIEST: Anyway, in addition to these exciting acts, do you do other things?

PENITENT: Why shouldn't I?

PRIEST: Does your husband force you to take up any special positions that humiliate you?

PENITENT: I think that the search for pleasure can never be humiliating if done with love.

PRIEST: It depends, my child. Does he make you turn over for lascivious purposes?

PENITENT: Well, I don't know, I can't stand that word lascivious. We're husband and wife, we love each other, and we try to love each other in the most complete way. I have nothing else to say, Father.

PRIEST: Calm down, my child, we must ... you must talk about these things, if you want to know what is good and what is bad. [*Pause*] For instance, does he use—do you use sadistic methods, a mirror, or other things of that kind?

PENITENT: Listen, Father, I don't want to know what's good or bad. I came here only to ask you whether, in being with my husband in certain ways, I can consider myself Catholic and take Communion. Please answer that question.

PRIEST: You see, if I've asked you these things, it's because I wanted to help you to understand yourself better. It's harder for a confessor to hear certain things than it is for a penitent to say them, believe me, my child. [*Pause*] You know, one hears the most incredible things in the confessional, one becomes hardened to them. Anyway, I understand you, don't worry. You're good at heart and I believe that you behave well with your husband. Don't go too far, but don't draw back either, because otherwise you might lose him. Rest assured, you're not in the least outside the Church and you may certainly take Communion. But you must confess at least once a month and try to come always to the same confessor, with whom you can establish a relationship of confidence such as can permit you to open up completely and thus have the most useful and honest help. Do you understand, my child?

PENITENT: I thank you, Father.

PRIEST: Now, say three Hail Marys to Our Lady and the Act of Contrition.


CHURCH OF SANTA CHIARA, ROME

PRIEST: How long is it since you confessed?

PENITENT: About a month, I think.

PRIEST: What sins have you committed?

PENITENT: You see, Father, I really want to ask your advice. I'm married and relations with my wife had been a bit strained for some time. We don't arrive at orgasm together. So maybe that's the reason. We were both brought up very strictly as Christians and maybe this prevents us from having relations in a natural way. There's a sort of feeling of guilt if we engage in some actions that are, well, a bit daring. Is it a sin to let oneself be guided by one's imagination and seek certain kinds of sexual excitement?

PRIEST: Of course it's not a sin, my son. Why do you think that?

PENITENT: Well, I've always been told—

PRIEST: Never mind what you've been told. It's true there are still some priests who've remained in the Middle Ages, but it no longer makes sense. You're running a big risk of wrecking your marriage because of stupidities.

PENITENT: So, then, can we do all the things we feel like doing?

PRIEST: Sure. But you must take care not to go too far, not to burn up your nervous energies too quickly, after having repressed them for so long. It will not be easy for your wife, either, to free herself from the guilt feelings caused by mistaken modesty. You're the one who will have to help her, lead her little by little into a relationship, a full one, that completes and satisfies you both, do you understand? It needs tact, patience, altruism and faith in God, much faith, my son.

PENITENT: But what is permissible, and what is not, for a good Christian?

PRIEST: Everything that serves to prepare for intercourse is permissible. It's not permissible to break off intercourse halfway through and complete it outside the natural place. Do you understand?

PENITENT: But isn't enjoyment of one's own body sinful?

PRIEST: No, it's not sinful if it's accompanied by love and is within the framework of a Christian marriage, do you see? Today there are publications that are very well done, which tell how two married Catholics should behave. Read it. Read one together with your wife, and have no further fears.

PENITENT: Thank you, Father.

PRIEST: It won't be easy, because I understand your case very well indeed. Nowadays, most young people don't have these problems. They know only too well how to act with their wives —and even with their fiancées—and even with any girl, unfortunately. And it's a fine thing that you and your wife still cloak your relations with so much modesty. But be careful, or else you'll find yourself estranged from the society in which you live. Sexual stimuli are natural things, they're not sinful, just so long as they take place within marriage that is blessed by God. If you wish, suggest to your wife that she come have a talk with me. I'll try to help her, remove the mistaken ideas she has about sex. When you're in bed, you must relax, abandon yourselves to whatever you feel like doing, without complexes, without mistaken modesty. You're husband and wife, aren't you? Undress her, caress her, kiss her, wherever you like, wherever you feel like doing it, see? Make her feel like a woman and you'll see that she responds to your urgings. The only thing you have to bear in mind is that the culmination of pleasure, if it's not to be sinful, if it's to be Christian, must be experienced by both of you together in your wife's vagina, do you understand? Now, son, say a Hail Mary and an Our Father and a Gloria for penance.

### Church of Santa Croce in Gerusalemme, Rome

PRIEST: Jesus Christ be praised.

PENITENT: May He always be praised.

PRIEST: How long has it been since you confessed?

PENITENT: Oh, seven or eight months.

PRIEST: What have you been doing in the meantime?

PENITENT: Father, I have a problem. I've only been married a few years, but my husband now wants to . . . wants to do things with me that he never did before and I—

PRIEST: Don't like it very much!

PENITENT: I don't know if I ought—

PRIEST: To continue?

PENITENT: Well, if I ought to allow it or—

PRIEST: What do these things consist of, these offenses against marriage?

PENITENT: I don't know.

PRIEST: Perhaps they're very delicate things, against conception?

PENITENT: I don't know.

PRIEST: Exactly.

PENITENT: I'm ashamed to speak of them.

PRIEST: Well, do they offend your dignity as a woman or are they just against insemination? Or are they acts that Catholic morality judges to be improper?

PENITENT: Well, I don't know. That's what I want to find out.

PRIEST: Yes, well, are these improper acts connected with the marital union, say, or are they just sadistic?

PENITENT: I wouldn't say sadism. I don't know. What does sadism mean?

PRIEST: Sadism means to have irregular enjoyment, purely personal, that's all.

PENITENT: Well, I don't know, no. No. Because he has an orgasm and it's not that I don't enjoy it. But I don't know whether the Church—

PRIEST: I don't understand you. If you can make me understand, in some way . . . You see, we study, let's say, all sins, and we can establish immediately what your constriction is, whether it's a constriction that's less dignified or whether—

PENITENT: Ask me some questions.

PRIEST: As I've said, I'm a confessor and so . . . is it during the conjugal act or during preparation?

PENITENT: During the preparation.

PRIEST: So, he makes you touch things that are not right?

PENITENT: Yes, but also, for instance—

PRIEST: With the hands?

PRIEST: Yes, with the hands.

PRIEST: Perhaps at times there are these deviations with the mouth?

PENITENT: And that isn't allowed?

PRIEST: It's humiliating for a wife, isn't it? Because, you see, that way he puts his member into your mouth and forces you to do these—these irreverent things. Isn't it so?

PENITENT: Yes.

PRIEST: And he spills his seed in your mouth too, perhaps?

PENITENT: Yes.

PRIEST: Well, this is an illicit bestiality. Does he force you to do this often?

PENITENT: Well, now it's becoming something that—

PRIEST: A bestiality not approved by Christian morality because in this way he wishes to have his climax in the place that is not usual, so that for you, also, the act is difficult. It's also humiliating, is it not?

PENITENT: But why is it humiliating? I don't understand.

PRIEST: It's humiliating in that it's not a suitable place to receive the orgasm.

PENITENT: Father, what I want to know is whether it's a sin or not.

PRIEST: You are an accomplice in your husband's impure act, aren't you? For example, if, after becoming excited he were to put his organ into your natural place and were to pour his seed into it, you would not be an accomplice, it would just be an exaggerated form of excitement. On the other hand, when he comes outside the natural place, in your mouth or else outside, etc., you are an accomplice in your husband's impure act.

PENITENT: So, must I confess every time I intend to take Communion?

PRIEST: Well, let us understand each other. If your husband persists in this you can say to yourself, "I want to estrange myself from this act." You can now pass as a passive person who is constricted. I don't know whether you understand me.

PENITENT: In that case I wouldn't be—

PRIEST: You wouldn't be guilty, because you would say, "I am constricted," and it's as if freedom were to be taken away from a person, forcibly. On the other hand, if you can repress this act of bestiality on the part of your husband, then you can set your conscience to rest.

PENITENT: But I daren't refuse him, because then he might look elsewhere for what he can't have with me.

PRIEST: Well, madam, I don't think so. These expedients that often happen are acts of bestiality, of exaggeration.

PENITENT: Why bestiality? It's a natural thing too, isn't it?

PRIEST: A natural thing? The natural thing is for the member to be in the female's sexual parts, but it's not a natural thing for it to be in the mouth. This can be an act of excitement for those who are cold but it's not—it's not consonant with nature.

PENITENT: So, it is permissible as preparation?

PRIEST: As preparation it can be allowed, yes. You must remain within these terms, right? In any case, such preparations are exaggerated because in conjugal life there are all those tricks in order to get excited and to be able to carry out the conjugal act and to be able to love each other mutually and in joint accord. But there is an exaggerated form of excitement, of corporal enjoyment, which is called bestiality. That is, only the beasts, who do not understand, have these remedies. And yet the beasts are wiser than men, are they not? Courage, courage. Unfortunately, you see, we confessors and you penitents must talk about these things which are done, unfortunately, and one feels ... uncomfortable about confessing them. So, take courage. Try to moralize as far as possible. And then, I have given you absolution, so there. Can you remember anything else?

PENITENT: No, no.

PRIEST: You always come to mass?

PENITENT: Yes.

PRIEST: Do you try to say your prayers?

PENITENT: Yes, when I have the time.

PRIEST: Since you have made a good confession, let us hope that you will make a good Communion. Be strong enough to keep your faith steady, keep your home the sanctuary of the family, a sanctuary that must always burn with faith, hope, and love. For penance say three Hail Marys and three Glorias to Our Lady. Now recite the Act of Contrition.

*Here are the more interesting extracts from other recorded conversations also based on this type of situation.*

CHURCH OF SAN GIORGIO, SALERNO

PENITENT: You see, Father, recently habit has worn out the physical attraction between me and my wife, so that now, for some time, before performing the sexual act, we seek new forms of excitement. I wanted to know whether the Church considers this a sin. How far can a Catholic couple go without falling into sin?

PRIEST: Kisses, caresses, touching each other, those are not sins. All the rest, yes. And the sin is all the graver if it's done with malice, that is, to obtain an excitement that isn't strictly necessary for performance of the sexual act.

PENITENT: I see.

PRIEST: In short, between married couples, all those acts that facilitate the performance of the conjugal act are permissible. Whether they come before or after. Up to complete satisfaction, right? On the other hand, acts against nature are not permissible, those that are used to avoid birth. You understand, don't you? Other acts against nature.

PENITENT: What do you mean by acts against nature, Father?

PRIEST: Acts of sodomy, for instance. Do you understand? And also avoiding having children with malicious intent on the part of the two partners.

PENITENT: But we already have two children and we don't want to have any more, Father. It's inevitable that we should try to . . . avoid the complete sexual act, isn't it?

PRIEST: Well, it's not necessary to intend making children every time you carry out your marital duties. But it's necessary, at least, that the act should take place in a normal manner.

PENITENT: In what sense?

PRIEST: So often, between married people, between certain couples, some acts of sodomy occur. And when copulation is understood exclusively in that way, as an end in itself, it's a sin. Do you understand?

SAN MARTINO CATHEDRAL, LUCCA

PENITENT: Father, there are other things besides the conjugal act.

PRIEST: What things, for instance? Kisses, embraces, caresses, getting close to each other's bodies, all these are permissible because they can also serve for the preparation of the conjugal act. Of course, my daughter, if they're really indecent things—

PENITENT: Well, I don't know whether they're indecent or not.

PRIEST: Moderate acts like embraces and kisses, I've already told you, are all permissible for married people. They are, in short, those things that are legitimized by the sacrament of matrimony and serve to prepare oneself bodily for the conjugal act and to nourish love.

PENITENT: But it can happen sometimes that—

PRIEST: You see, if a thing is to be a sin, it must be done with conviction, be really desired. Of course, if one sets out with certain intentions, deliberately, well, then, yes, it would be a bit sinful. But, on the other hand, if that's what your husband wants!

PENITENT: Yes, all right, but am I committing a sin?

PRIEST: But you, inside yourself, before God, must show plainly that you're prepared to accept everything as a sacrifice, but that you desire His grace.

PENITENT: It's not a question of sacrifice. I'm too shy, I'm ashamed.

PRIEST: In such cases, it's not a question of being ashamed. There must be no shame between husband and wife. If anything, you must think that if he were to go and seek other women, it would be worse, wouldn't it? You, then, must lend yourself, as I've told you, almost as if you were an instrument, without worrying yourself about it.

CHIESA NUOVA SANTA MARIA VALICELLA, ROME

PENITENT: As I told you, Father, when I was thirteen years old I didn't know how babies were born because sex was taboo. So I found myself in difficulties with my husband later, and now I don't know whether—whether it's a problem I should confess or, at least, whether or not I've committed sins.

PRIEST: But toward your children, madam, in the future, don't have any taboos. Begin—I don't know how old they are but they must be very small because you're young—begin as soon as you can, and explain certain problems to them.

PENITENT: Yes, indeed, but it's very difficult. The fact that, when I used to go to Catholic Action, sex and relations between men and women were always considered sinful on principle, and to my mind, that too is wrong.

PRIEST: But a lot of progress has been made, you know. A great deal.

PENITENT: My problem is that my husband expects or asks for sexual manifestations, let's say, and I don't know if they're permissible. I don't know whether they're sinful or not, that's it.

PRIEST: Look, you can't ask me a question of that kind because I don't have an automatic reply to whatever it is you do. I can give you some principles. I think you're a good and intelligent woman. You mustn't do this or that thing while wondering whether it's a sin or not. There are states of conscience, some very grave problems that have to be looked at very clearly. Let me explain. The fact that you, husband and wife, love each other and have had some sexual satisfaction is very beautiful and holy because you love each other just for this reason. However, one has to view it clearly as a human action. You must not be a male or female who meet and let themselves go, because in that case you would be two beasts. Have I made myself clear?

PENITENT: Yes.

PRIEST: In your relations as man and wife you must have an

evaluation. Pay attention to me, because these things that I'm telling you are very important. You must respect each other. Respect means that the man must not enjoy himself and let himself go with his woman as if she were an object to be enjoyed. The woman would probably feel humiliated. This is immoral. It's necessary, therefore, that the relationship between you should truly be a relation of love. In other words the physical act should not be a physical outlet, but the expression of a whole set of lovely things that exist between a man and a woman. I don't know if I've made myself clear.

PENITENT: Yes, I understand. But up to what point is it not sinful?     1802992

PRIEST: It is not I who establish sin. Sin is committed in one's own conscience. This is something that must stop. One should not ask another person, "Am I sinning?" It's not another person who can tell you if you're sinning.

PENITENT: But there are some rules which, if one breaks them, one falls into sin, isn't that so?

PRIEST: Confession isn't regulated by a civil or penal code.

PENITENT: But up till now I've always heard phrases like "God's law says so and that's enough."

PRIEST: But how many laws of God exist that you don't even know about? How many laws of God exist that don't concern you at all? These laws of God must become the laws that govern your conscience. God's law isn't something exterior, hung on the wall, that I can look at to see whether I'm doing good or evil. God's law passes through the conscience. There's no God that forces you to have children, you know. There's no one that can say to you, "Every time you sleep with your husband, you must make a child." There's no law of God that says, "You are husband and wife and you mustn't have any kind of sexual relations." There's no law of God that says that.

CHURCH OF SANTA MARIA DEGLI ANGELI, SAN REMO

PRIEST: How long is it since you confessed?

PRIEST: I don't know exactly.

PRIEST: Months, perhaps?

PENITENT: Yes.

PRIEST: Do you go to mass on Sundays?

PENITENT: Yes.

PRIEST: Do you say your prayers at night?

PENITENT: Yes, surely.

PRIEST: Do you ever tell lies?

PENITENT: No.

PRIEST: Acts of impatience, intemperance?

PENITENT: No. Listen, the problem is ... I haven't been married long.

PRIEST: Yes?

PENITENT: And my husband, I don't know ... he does things to me, we do things.

PRIEST: Normal things?

PENITENT: That's the point. I mean, am I committing a sin, or not?

PRIEST: Well, you do perform the conjugal act, don't you?

PENITENT: Yes, but other things too. I don't know whether it's sinful or not.

PRIEST: We'll have to see if they're things against nature, because if they are, it's sinful. But if they're normal things, the normal conjugal act, it's not sinful, it's permitted.

PENITENT: I don't know, exactly, whether they're normal or not.

PRIEST: Before the act itself you do things?

PENITENT: Well, yes.

PRIEST: Then, do you perform the sexual act in the vagina or in the back part?

PENITENT: I don't know—well, in both.

PRIEST: In both? Do you consent to that thing from behind, I mean in the back part?

PENITENT: I leave it to my husband.

PRIEST: But what do you prefer, the vagina or your behind?

PENITENT: I don't know. I feel pleasure in both cases.

PRIEST: Both. You mean you consent to both, of course. Is that true?

PENITENT: Well, what should I do?

PRIEST: Of course, in performing that act with a part of the body that is not—not pertinent, you may be doing something which may also be harmful to your health. Do you understand? Because the sexual act is normally performed in the vagina. But if you've done so, you must be very careful because it's abnormal, from a medical point of view as well. If you had to pass a medical examination, an open vagina is of no importance, but the anal orifice—it means that you've done things against nature you should not have done. Do you understand?

PENITENT: Yes.

PRIEST: On the other hand, if your husband insists, if he really wants to do it that way, he has absolute rights over the woman's body. So therefore—

PENITENT: There is one thing I don't understand. Don't I have absolute rights over *his* body?

PRIEST: Yes, you do. In this concept the needs of the husband blend with those of the wife and those of the wife with those of the husband. However, these are not normal things. You realize that, eh?

PENITENT: I don't know. Which things are permissible and which are not?

PRIEST: Well, it's permissible for a married couple to embrace, to kiss, to touch each other, to excite each other in preparation for the act—all this is permissible. But the complete sexual act is when the husband releases his seed in his wife's vagina, you understand? Then it is complete. But you don't do this, do you? Is it because you don't want children?

PENITENT: Not for the moment.

PRIEST: And so your husband tries to avoid it, right?

PENITENT: Yes.

PRIEST: Exactly. And do you use—that is, does your husband use—illicit things to prevent his seed from going into the vagina, or does he just withdraw and that's all?

PENITENT: It depends, sometimes one way and sometimes the other.

PRIEST: And you? Do you sometimes help him in taking care— Certainly this is not sinful. It's sinful only when children are voluntarily and directly avoided by illicit means. Do you understand? If, for instance, you douche. If the man withdraws before having expelled his seed, with the intention of not having children, then he's obliged to confess this. All the rest is permissible between married people, do you understand? The act that is not normal and unnatural is the one performed in the anus. It's not permissible because it is against nature, do you see? Now, it *is* permissible if the wife consents and it's the husband who asks her for it. Both have to be in agreement, do you understand? But, it's always an action against nature, it's not normal. Do you understand?

PENITENT: Yes.

PRIEST: All right. Try to be good. Have you always been faithful to your husband? Have you loved him?

PENITENT: Yes.

PRIEST: Try to pour out all your affection toward your husband, and also to have some children, do you understand? And thus you will have greater blessings from Our Lord. Try to pray, to endure, with the greatest possible serenity, everything that life brings you, to stay close to Our Lady, so that Our Lord and Our Lady can help you and direct all the spiritual and material needs that you may have in the right direction. Eh?

PENITENT: Yes, Father.

PRIEST: Now, ask forgiveness for all the sins you have committed and say three Hail Marys to Our Lady. Recite the Act of Contrition.

## CONCLUSION: LOVE PLAY, YES, BUT ONLY AS A PRELIMINARY STEP

According to the priests, love play is permissible, indeed necessary, as long as it is preparatory to the complete sexual act—aimed, that is, at procreation. Otherwise, love play is sinful.

Three aspects in the above confessions are worth making special note of. First, most of the priests (50 out of 96) seem more curious about superfluous details than they should be. They push the penitent to use concrete terms and describe the complete mechanism of love play, especially when the penitent is a woman. This approach of the priest seems to border on morbidity and may well do nothing more than show the frustration of the one who sits behind the confessional.

Second is the confusion of some of the priests. One, for instance, disapproves of certain confessed deviations when they are first mentioned but ends up accepting them.

The third aspect is the most important. The Church, as far as sexual relations between married people are concerned, has stated that the times are past when the husband wanted a docile and submissive wife. The Church now seems to encourage preparatory acts. The priests suggest that women become inventive in their love play and that brides, especially, must learn that modesty doesn't fit in with the matrimonial atmosphere. The conjugal relations should be imbued, according to one priest, "with every possible shade of novelty." And, contrary to past teaching, some representatives of the Church were saying that "the aim of the sexual act need not necessarily be procreation."

The problem is that not all the priests have gone forward at the same pace. Other priests still claim that love play is right only when it prepares the couple for procreative intercourse.

No wonder many Catholics are confused by their Church's stance.

# II

## SEXUAL RELATIONS BETWEEN ENGAGED COUPLES

THE SECOND typical situation used in these conversations in the confessional is that of a young engaged couple who have not performed intercourse but would like to do so or, at least, know what the limits are for premarital lovemaking.

In any age in which psychology has removed many of the taboos from sexuality, the Church's stand confuses many young people. Psychologists on the whole favor intimacy between teen-agers. They say that it is damaging to a young person's psyche to inhibit his sexual drive and then suddenly free himself when he marries. Such an approach is, according to one psychologist, "a glaring piece of contradiction which can bring about irreparable shock to the matrimonial ménage."

What is the stand taken by the priest? To establish this, we recorded one hundred confessions. The priests stated unanimously that the Church cannot permit any premarital intercourse. On the question of what two young people *can* do before marriage, there were some differences. The majority allowed kissing "like brother and sister," but only fourteen consider other types of caresses not sinful.

40

## UNCOMPROMISING CONFESSORS

*The large majority of the priests, 86 per cent, took an extremely rigid stand on premarital relations. We quote the most representative conversations.*

CHURCH OF SAN FRANCESCO, PISTOIA

PRIEST: How long has it been since your last confession?
PENITENT: About six months.
PRIEST: What sins have you committed?
PENITENT: The problem is I've gotten engaged and I'm having trouble with my fiancé. I quarrel with him because he'd like . . . he asks me to do things that I'm not sure are permitted.
PRIEST: Are they things against morality, against your conscience?
PENITENT: They're things that are natural and . . . I don't know . . .
PRIEST: Natural things? What is natural between husband and wife, isn't natural between unmarried people. That's the moral law.
PENITENT: Yes, but he says we should know each other from the sexual point of view, so as to avoid mistakes after we're married.
PRIEST: These are your fiancé's ideas that don't match those of Christian morality. Anyone can think what he wants, but he can't pretend it's God's will, can he? If you believe, if you want to follow Christian morality, this is no longer natural.
PENITENT: I don't know. The fact that a woman and a man go together, that they have certain feelings and that they have to repress them continually seems less natural to me.
PRIEST: No, it isn't that they have to—
PENITENT: What?

PRIEST: It's not that they have to repress them. Marriage exists especially for this.

PENITENT: That's right, but we're not married yet.

PRIEST: Well, then, be patient a little while longer. Wait until the right time for these things.

PENITENT: But still, a priest once—he was a foreigner—told me that it wasn't a serious sin for engaged couples to have intercourse.

PRIEST: Well, having intercourse, that is, committing the sexual act, is a serious sin, it's committing an impure act.

PENITENT: Yes, all right, but there are things . . . maybe it's all right if it isn't complete intercourse.

PRIEST: You can't split hairs about the act, complete or otherwise. Even desire, sexual desire alone, is already a sin.

PENITENT: But between two people who love each other, who are attracted to each other, it happens naturally.

PRIEST: But it's not—

PENITENT: You say that even desire is a sin.

PRIEST: —it's not the desire for a thing. It's something that will be right at the right time but is illicit at the moment. Engagement is nothing but preparation for marriage, isn't it, and it must be seen from this point of view.

PENITENT: But shouldn't it also be preparation from the sexual point of view?

PRIEST: If you make such statements, don't come here to argue against Christian morality.

PENITENT: I think that all sorts of things happen between young people these days.

PRIEST: Well, a lot of robberies, murders, and other crimes take place, too, but that doesn't mean they're right!

PENITENT: You can't put those acts on the same level as—

PRIEST: No, reasoning like that we *are* putting them on the same level.

PENITENT: But relations between the sexes aren't the same as they were fifty years ago.

PRIEST: It's a depravation of common morality.

PENITENT: Would you be more in favor of engaged couples never meeting alone, the way things happened, for instance, in our parents' time, when someone else always had to be present? I don't think that today—

PRIEST: Yes, there's more freedom between the sexes, but this freedom should be viewed as a trust, not as an opportunity to take advantage.

PENITENT: You say engagement is a preparation for marriage. Well, I know some couples who are separated now just because they didn't get along sexually, and I'm determined— I don't know, it may be a selfish fixation, but I'd like to avoid making their mistake, which came about because they didn't know each other before marriage, sexually, that is.

PRIEST: But sexual preparation doesn't mean using sexuality for one's own pleasure. That's no preparation.

PENITENT: I mean getting to know one another in this way too.

PRIEST: So you have an unsanctioned marriage, don't you, eh?

PENITENT: But would it be better, according to the Church and Christian morality as you say, for me to get married, for instance, and then not get along with my husband? Because two people are made in a certain way and it might very well be that we might not match. That's possible, isn't it?

PRIEST: Why do you consider everything from the sexual angle?

PENITENT: Not everything, but from that angle *as well*. Sex is an important part of marriage.

PRIEST: Yes, but it's not a part about which one should make such a fuss.

PENITENT: It's not a question of making a fuss. Since I've seen examples, friends of my mother's . . . well, I'm afraid. I really am. Since the Church doesn't allow divorce, if we don't get along once we're married, what kind of life would we have?

PRIEST: Even divorce wouldn't solve your problem.

PENITENT: But it's better to avoid making a mistake before an indissoluble marriage, isn't it?

PRIEST: But you can't base your life on an initial sin, can you?

PENITENT: Sin? What sin?

PRIEST: Sin is sexual intercourse between people who aren't married. But if you don't believe this, then—

PENITENT: No, it's just that I want to understand why it's a sin, since it's a natural thing. Who are we hurting, may I ask?

PRIEST: You're hurting yourselves. Because the act is meant for the procreation of children, and to perform it without procreating children, that's already something unnatural.

PENITENT: Yes, but even the Church now admits that in marriage the act isn't just for procreation. You know that.

PRIEST: That's not true, the Church hasn't yet admitted anything.

PENITENT: But I read that the Pope himself said it, it wasn't me who said it.

PRIEST: No matter, the natural fact is that this act is meant for the preservation of the species. Now, two people who have no guarantee of a life in common cannot perform it, because if they keep children from being brought into the world by various means . . . but these are perversions of natural law. You say that no one is being harmed. But that's no justification.

PENITENT: Anyway, if my boy friend asks me to do it—

PRIEST: Look, if you have faith in Christian morality, you know how you must behave. If, on the other hand, you're not convinced—

PENITENT: And if then he makes love with other women?

PRIEST: Look, he can do that in any case.

PENITENT: That's what you say, Father.

PRIEST: There are lots of husbands who make love with their wives and also with other women! So that doesn't resolve the problem. Meantime, if he goes with others, it could mean that he doesn't have good intentions toward you. To say, "I only want you if you'll go with me sexually, otherwise I'll go with someone else"—what kind of honesty is that?

PENITENT: Well, no, there are certain physiological needs that can't be repressed.

PRIEST: That's his affair. If he hasn't accustomed himself, he has no moral sense concerning his own existence. When a person is brought up badly, he cannot justify his sinful requirements, not from a moral point of view. It's wrong from the start. People have become outlaws in this way. We can't justify him, we must change him!

PENITENT: I see. Well, all right. What can I allow him to do? Up to what point? Is kissing a sin too?

PRIEST: Kissing is not a sin. It has never been.

PENITENT: But I mean—not a brotherly kiss.

PRIEST: Yes, yes, I understand. The kisses that engaged people give each other, on the mouth. Yes, so long as they don't last an hour. Because then they can excite sexual instincts. But an affectionate kiss, even an expansive one, so long as it's affectionate, is not sinful. A caress too, so long as one doesn't descend to things . . . to things that sometimes go straight into bestiality that excites the sexual instincts. Then they become an opportunity for getting excited and lead to sin. You see, with regard to faith and morality, it's not that we are obliged to follow others. If we are not convinced, Our Lord doesn't oblige anyone. Salvation is for everyone, but God never forces anyone. This is the way. Do you wish to follow it? If you don't, leave the Church. I shall be sorry for you, and I will find a way, sooner or later, to call you back. Remember that God is for everyone, but there is no justification for sin.

PENITENT: All right, Father, thank you for explaining things to me.

Como Cathedral

PRIEST: May Jesus Christ be praised.

PENITENT: May He always be praised.

PRIEST: How long is it since your last confession?

PENITENT: Well, about three months.

PRIEST: Three months? Why so long?

PENITENT: I don't know. Perhaps ... I don't know ... I'm going through a bit of a crisis, Father. I came not so much to make a confession, but for some advice.

PRIEST: Very well. Tell me about it.

PENITENT: I'm engaged and my fiancé and I have decided to have sexual relations. I thought that if we do this, I would find myself cut off from the Church. This is my problem, Father.

PRIEST: Certainly if you make a decision like that so deliberately, you will lose the grace of God, my dear child. Have you already had intercourse?

PENITENT: No, not yet. At least not completely.

PRIEST: Did you in any case go beyond the limits of what is permissible?

PENITENT: What do you mean, Father? I don't know what these limits are for the Church.

PRIEST: Did you go further than kissing?

PENITENT: Well, yes.

PRIEST: Tell me, child, what you have done?

PENITENT: The things you do when you go with someone. The usual things.

PRIEST: Caresses?

PENITENT: Yes, Father.

PRIEST: Is it he alone who does these things, my dear child?

PENITENT: Yes ... well, both of us.

PRIEST: But do you caress each other without ill intent, with affection, or do you caress lasciviously?

PENITENT: But, Father, I've never thought of it that way. We do it instinctively, because we love each other.

PRIEST: I mean, does he touch your delicate parts—your breasts, your sex?

PENITENT: What does that matter?

PRIEST: A great deal, my dear child, a great deal. Because caresses of this kind are lascivious, nothing to do with the love you feel for each other.

PENITENT: Are these things sins?

PRIEST: Of course. And most serious ones.

PENITENT: So then . . .

PRIEST: But do you touch him everywhere?

PENITENT: Yes.

PRIEST: Only with your hands, or with your mouth as well?

PENITENT: Father, I feel embarrassed talking about these things. We don't feel we're doing anything wrong. Love is made of these things as well and we love each other. This is why I haven't been to confession for so long. I had thought that you would condemn these things, whereas we don't see anything unclean in them . . . for us it's something natural. As it is for almost all engaged couples.

PRIEST: My dear child, these are not natural things, as you put it. These contacts, these caresses, are permissible only if they serve as a preparation to the full sexual act, and you cannot engage in the complete sexual act until you have been united in a proper family bond through marriage.

PENITENT: I don't understand.

PRIEST: The fact that you caress and kiss your fiancé's sex is not—how can I put it?—a demonstration of affection, but a bestial excitement of the senses, do you understand? It stimulates a bestial instinct that leads animals to procreation. But you cannot procreate, because you are not husband and wife. Or perhaps you would like to have a child?

PENITENT: We don't want to have children now. We simply

wish to enrich our love with a further experience. Father, do you consider marriage a serious matter?

PRIEST: I should think so!

PENITENT: And since we too consider it a serious thing, we want to come to it after having, after being absolutely certain whether or not there can be physical harmony between us.

PRIEST: But God cannot allow this, my dear child. You have already seriously overstepped the boundaries of Christian love, giving yourself over to the crudest instincts of your fiancé, and releasing in yourself these same instincts. Did you not feel ashamed—your modesty as a virgin—when the hands and the mouth of your fiancé explored your naked body exposed to his lust? And you yourself did these same things to him, contributing to his excitement and perhaps to the scattering of his seed. Did this ever happen during these sessions of yours?

PENITENT: Well, yes.

PRIEST: And did you bring him to this point by your touching?

PENITENT: When, we love, we love reciprocally, Father.

PRIEST: But God does not want this to happen, my dear child. Only within the sacrament of marriage is orgasm—the act of procreation—permitted. You are free to behave as you think best, but you can't expect God to approve your pleasing of yourself.

PENITENT: Well, Father, this was what I wanted to know. I don't believe that having intercourse with my fiancé is a matter of pleasing myself. I think instead that's it's something natural that happens. It's not as if I had fallen into his arms the first day we met, without even knowing who he was. A fairly solid bond of affection exists between us.

PRIEST: My child, we have no possibility of understanding each other. God has given us laws, and you want me to authorize you to disobey them! That cannot be done!

PENITENT: But, Father, you say that it is not even permitted to express affection without the sexual act.

PRIEST: No, I didn't say that, my child. I said we cannot allow gestures which go too far, which are lascivious, you understand? So you will not feel the temptation to have complete intercourse. If it is from affection, you can very well caress each other, kiss—on the face, that is.

PENITENT: I understand. The fact is that once the Church wouldn't allow even a kiss between sweethearts, and now some things are allowed. I thought there was not clear division between what is permissible and what isn't. I mean, that these limits were to be set by the good faith and the conscience of the person involved.

PRIEST: The Church, my dear child, cannot set laws case by case. That would be a fine state of affairs!

PENITENT: I understand. But the priest might have the faculty of judging each case on its own merits, don't you think?

PRIEST: No, no. I don't know. You may be right in this, but at present I have no authority to do as you ask, my dear child. Therefore, if you promise to go back on your decision and resolve to behave properly with your fiancé, I can give you absolution.

PENITENT: All right, Father, thank you very much. I'll think it over.

PRIEST: Yes, my child, think it over and come back. It will always do you good to talk, to confide in someone. In the meantime, I give you God's blessing.


CHURCH OF SANT 'AGOSTINO, MODENA

PRIEST: How long is it since your last confession?

PENITENT: About three months.

PRIEST: What sins have you committed?

PENITENT: I find myself in a certain situation. You see, it's not so much that I want to confess myself, but that I want your opinion on a problem I have.

PRIEST: What is it about?

PENITENT: I'm engaged, and my girl friend ... well, we've

decided to have full intercourse, because we want to get to know each other fully before tying ourselves down definitely by marriage.

PRIEST: But that's not possible!

PENITENT: Why not?

PRIEST: Because Christian morality doesn't permit it. The idea of wanting to get to know each other better is just a nice excuse for satisfying your desires, isn't that so? You ought, rather, to have a sense of responsibility, a conscience. I say again, no intimate contacts of the kind that can be permissible only in marriage. There can, of course, be expressions of love . . . of affection. . . .

PENITENT: But what kind of lovemaking is permitted, that is, not considered sinful?

PRIEST: Kissing is permitted.

PENITENT: Well, that's something! Once not even that was allowed.

PRIEST: But it may be, as they say, a chaste kiss. And some embraces. Just so long as everything . . . you see . . . is done with proper intentions. The kiss, the embrace, must not be something that satisfies your desires, your exigencies. Only actions that serve to manifest the love that you feel for each other.

PENITENT: I'm sorry, Father, but I don't understand that. Life today is different from what it was. No one but a saint dreams of accepting these criteria regarding sin. It seems to me that the Church is making a mistake in not keeping up with the times. I feel completely confused. I'm a Catholic, I believe that basically I'm good, I admire certain spiritual values, I would like to be . . . I mean I'd like to live in peace with God, but with these rules that you offer me, I can't do it. I'd feel like someone estranged from the society all around me. I thank you, Father, for what you've told me, but I don't believe that a man must pay such a high price, and one that makes no logical sense, to call himself a Christian.

PRIEST: You're saying things that make no sense, my son. I can understand your state of mind, troubled by passion . . . but you're making a mistake. Matrimony is a sacred thing, you must not contaminate it—in the name of civilization and progress—by actions that Christ Himself described as sins. How many times has society in the past acted in a way contrary to the principles of the Church, as it is acting now? But then, the Church has always proved to be right in the end. The safeguarding of the family, opposed nowadays by almost everyone, is a duty that the Church performs and one that everyone will thank it for later on, my son. You can be sure of that!

PENITENT: Let's leave aside the fact that it's always been the Church that has had to give way to the times, although I think that the Church ought to move *with* the times so as to be able to offer its valid experience. This isn't the time and place for that. Let's get back to my problem. I think that a person like me, who has decided to have intercourse with his fiancée, after being engaged for a certain period, and with a sense of responsibility which I claim, right here in the confessional, can't be written off as just a "sinner," period! There should be recognition of his wish to be fully convinced, before tying himself and another person down, that this other person could have a chance of living happily with him for her whole life, from every point of view. Am I wrong?

PRIEST: I don't know. Look, you're free to do whatever you like. I merely tell you that the Church, which interprets the will of God, has precise rules which must be respected and I, as a priest, must do everything I can to see that this is done. If you want to paw your fiancée's body in order to feel—or rather to understand, as you put it—whether you both like it or not, that's your own affair.

PENITENT: I'm sorry, Father, if I've wasted your time, but I'd better go now. I dislike hearing the word "paw" used, and also the rest of your reasoning, which cheapens something that's really a serious matter. If you believe, and it's obvious you do, that what I've said to you is just an excuse for having intercourse with my fiancée, you're making a very big mistake. If that were so, I most certainly would never have come here to speak to you!

PRIEST: I'm sorry, but you see ... [*long pause*] you see, our position is not easy. It may be that you—no, undoubtedly you *are* acting in good faith, but there are so many others who are not. The Church has to take this into account, to consider the majority of people, because if it were to open the floodgate, all of them would take advantage and do just as they please—to do filthy things, you understand?

PENITENT: The Church could begin to consider its flock with less pessimism, don't you think, Father?

PRIEST: I don't think it's a question of pessimism. All we have to do is look around us. However, you must also think about the consequences of your action for the girl. She gives you her virginity, doesn't she? And then? If you were to discover that you're not made for each other? You, my son, suffer no consequences, but that poor girl will not be the same as she was before. Have you thought of this?

PENITENT: Excuse me, Father, but what if we found out that we were not made for each other *after* marriage? Would that be better? Could I come to you, then, to ask for a divorce? Wouldn't you answer that the Church doesn't allow it and that I ought to have thought of that before getting married? That's what I don't understand—whether the Church really wants to help people or whether it just wants to create difficulties and set up barriers. Anyway, Father, I'm sorry if I've wasted your time. Perhaps I had no right to do so. You see, I believe in God—I believe with conviction—but the God that I believe in has more respect for man and for human conscience.

PRIEST: You haven't wasted my time at all, my son, I'm here to listen to everyone. And to suffer too, my son, when I am unable, as in this case, to be a good intermediary between God and the penitent. Let's face it, we are in a period of great confusion, the Church is making a great effort to move with the times. Perhaps it doesn't fully succeed, but it has God behind it to inspire it, and so we must not despair. Do you understand, my son? Do you want to receive Communion?

PENITENT: I don't know, Father. I'd rather think over this talk we've had. Thank you, anyway.


CHURCH OF SAN CARLO AL CORSO, ROME

PRIEST: May Jesus Christ be praised.

PENITENT: May He always be praised.

PRIEST: What is it?

PENITENT: Father, I have a problem that I'd like to have your opinion on. I'm engaged and I can't control what my fiancé does any more. I don't know what to do. I know, you'll no doubt tell me that engaged people shouldn't ... shouldn't do certain things. . . .

PRIEST: It is not I. It's God's commandment that says so. It's Jesus Christ who says it, not the priest. We are Christians, and we have rules to observe, and these rules are Our Lord's commandments. The priests have absolutely nothing to do with it.

PENITENT: Yes, but look, once not even kissing was allowed, and now it is, so there has been a change, even in the evaluation of—

PRIEST: There is nothing new. Definitely not. I kiss my mother, I kiss my sister, let us suppose that I also kiss some good-looking girl that comes to see me. It all depends on the intention. You cannot blame the Church. The Church merely says, "Love each other, and love each other properly as you are supposed to love." Loving is never a sin when the rights of God are safeguarded. Now, if you kiss someone and begin to feel emotion, sentiment then, especially with kisses on the mouth which are unhygienic among other things, the sentiment is exactly the same as that of animals. If we do not dominate this sentiment, we end up possibly sinning mortally, gravely. Everything depends, my child, upon our intelligence, our will, in the observance of Our Lord's commandments, and so your problem is solved at once. If you are not able, through your intelligence and will, with the aid of Our Lord, to dominate yourself, it means that you are sinning, and that you are perhaps committing very grave sins.

PENITENT: I know, but there are two people, two bodies, not two pieces of wood, so that—

PRIEST: But you have intelligence, you have a will. When you are married, the two hearts will be one only. It all depends upon a proper understanding of Our Lord's words. The sixth and ninth commandments are for everyone—for me, for the Pope. Because we too are not pieces of wood, we too have a nature, my child.

PENITENT: I know, but you have chosen a path—

PRIEST: No, no, that has nothing to do with it, nothing at all. It's not the habit that makes the monk.

PENITENT: No, I mean—

PRIEST: Yes, but I—we, too, have our temptations. The devil does not leave anyone in peace. Indeed, we are perhaps more tempted than you are. But then, there is Our Lord's grace, Our Lord's help. There is prayer, there is our will so that we can say, "I have done this, therefore I must abstain from that." But now you, my child, you and your fiancé ... I always suggest this, because it is not just your problem, it is that of 80 per cent of young people ... I always suggest you must love each other and in the meantime meditate upon what love is. Now, it is not love that leads one into sin. You see, you yourself, this morning, come here to ask pardon for this thing. You have doubts, you don't know whether you have sinned and you begin to think up things like, "But the Church allows, but this, but that," which means there's something that isn't working, that is, your conscience, and your conscience, you know, is a fine thing that ought to tell you how far you can go with your fiancé. After all, what is an engagement for? To get to know each other.

PENITENT: Yes, I wanted to come to that—getting to know each other. But that means from a sexual point of view too, because if we don't get along sexually after we're married, what are we going to do? Separate?

PRIEST: Ah, and so you perform the act before getting married ... [*laughs ironically*] No, no.

PENITENT: But married life includes that too, and it's not the least important part.

PRIEST: But you can discuss it, there's no need to do these things!

PENITENT: What do you mean, discuss it? These things have to be felt, talking about them doesn't count.

PRIEST: No, no absolutely not. One can only discuss them. "I am marrying you because I wish to have children." If anything, the question you must ask yourself is, "Is he suitable for marriage, is he potent or impotent?" There's no need for any sort of test—*he* already knows.

PENITENT: Yes, but there could be incompatibility between us, couldn't there?

PRIEST: Certainly, but this incompatibility doesn't depend on the physical part.

PENITENT: How's that?

PRIEST: No! It depends on intelligence, my child.

PENITENT: On intelligence? I certainly don't believe that.

PRIEST: Yes, yes. Just study a little psychology and you'll see how things are. That's what I say, it may be that you're right, but I know from experience, from the first day I sat behind a confessional. I became a priest at twenty, so I know what life is about. I've always worked among young people, always in the parishes, and so in twenty years and more of the priesthood, experience means something, too. Now you come to me and ask me for an explanation and I give it to you as I feel it, because I've led many souls to marriage, and to many I've said, "No, you're not suitable for marriage." They've gotten married just the same and then they've come back to me and said, "Father, you were right. If only I'd listened to you I wouldn't find myself in this mess." And yet ...

PENITENT: Oh, well, those are problems of character, the ones you had evaluated. But there are also physical problems.

PRIEST: Physical ones, too. We had discussed that as well, even in the physiological field.

PENITENT: But I've seen the experiences of my friends, and of my mother too. It comes to a point where they don't get along with their husbands, sexually, and they have to separate. Why should I run this risk when—

PRIEST: So, you would commit a sin even before beginning your marriage?

PENITENT: But why is it a sin? I mean, it wouldn't be a sin if it were done with responsibility, would it?

PRIEST: No! Listen how she interprets Our Lord's law! I stand by what Our Lord's law says. The commandments don't say that you should test first to see if you're capable of conceiving.

PENITENT: And then, when people separate, you don't admit divorce . . .

PRIEST: Listen, I am telling you how things stand according to Catholic, Christian morality.

PENITENT: So, then, we have to repress nature, as you call it.

PRIEST: No, there isn't anything to repress. Let nature have its way.

PENITENT: And if nature pushes us in such a way that at a certain moment one person wants to have intercourse with the other?

PRIEST: Listen, these are things that have come to the fore only now, just because young people want to go further than . . . they think they're God. They no longer have faith in God, in God's commandments. None! Because there is only the case of physiological impotence, and in fact, to some I've said, go to a gynecologist, go to a doctor, have yourself examined. *Non sunt facenda mala ut degna bona*—one can't sin in order to obtain something good in the future. No! That is against morality.

PENITENT: Well then, what kind of relationship am I supposed to have with my fiancé?

PRIEST: The one your conscience dictates, my child. I don't

have anything to do with those things. We suggest that you should be careful because nature is weak, corruptible. Your nature is as corruptible as mine. And so things are done in haste, the heart cannot be commanded. This is where prayer comes in. The Lord is clear about this, "Without me you can do nothing." Do you want to do something good? Begin to pray for a start, to live your Christian life well, observing the sacred commandments of God. That's the first thing to do. The second thing is your will. Then, for the physiological part, let God attend to that. It is he who has created us. We have not created ourselves, you know.

PENITENT: Exactly. So if we have certain needs—

PRIEST: Let that be. When you feel these incitements toward union, which in themselves are not sinful because they are part of nature—well, if they didn't exist, no one would get married, because it's as if there were no enjoyment in eating, then no one would eat. It's the same for marriage. If there were not pleasure, the enjoyment of . . . this instinct, this law of integration, if this didn't exist, then no one would get married. No one. In the meantime, both of you examine your characters. Then, God will attend to what is to come. And anyway, even the fact of arriving at marriage still a virgin, for instance—

PENITENT: But everyone just laughs when I say these things.

PRIEST: Oh, the world today! Yes, yes, but in a hundred years' time we will see who will laugh. He who laughs last laughs best. There is terrible corruption today, you know, and because of it everyone wants to arrive quickly. A boy of sixteen or seventeen already wants to go with girls. And at twenty he really does. You see to what depths we have fallen? Where is morality? Where is the sense of modesty? Listen to me, child, and let the others laugh. You must have your own personality.

PENITENT: But among our friends all the engaged couples make love. It doesn't bother them at all.

PRIEST: Never mind the others! Why should you do what the others do? If they take the pill, cocaine—I don't know any of those things—do you have to take them too?

PENITENT: It's not the same thing at all, and you know it.

PRIEST: Yes, it is the same thing. Because he does that, I do it too. Like a flock of sheep—the first one goes and all the others follow. One must first have a personality! That's my answer to you. Then, you can do as you like. Anyway, you can kiss sometimes.

PENITENT: Ah! What kind of kisses?

PRIEST: I suggest a kiss when you meet and when you leave each other, in a friendly way, a pure kiss, not a sensual, carnal, emotional kiss—that's a bestial kiss, which not even beasts do. See how malicious man is? Where shall we end up? Only the flesh is considered and not the spirit. The values, the framework of values, are changing. We are not just bodies, we are intelligent, volitional beings. This is so, my child. If you want a fuller explanation, you must go to the confessor on my right here who is a psychologist and perhaps has studied more than I have. But we are all on the same plane. This is the truth. One has to be careful. I can't tell you kiss each other as you like. That is sinful. No one can check a kiss in view of our weak human nature, can they? And so we arrive at eroticism: complete eroticism. You are right when you say, "I am not a piece of wood." We are not pieces of wood either. Our natures, my child, are spoiled, ruined. That's why we must understand that a sin exists which ruins everything. But we also know that there is another person who has restored much of this human nature and today is the feast of Jesus' ascension to heaven. He ascends into heaven, in fact, after having tested our nature. And He says to us from up there, "Pray, dominate yourselves, control yourselves." Listen, my child, the gospel is there, and I cannot depart from the gospel. But you are free. I always say that I am free to go to paradise, just as I am free not to go there. God respects our personalities. But, the very fact that you have expressed your doubts to me here this morning is a fine proof of purity, it is grace received. Think about it. Anyway, I believe that when one really loves a person, love never leads to evil. This, I think, is the real definition of love.

PENITENT: Yes, Father. Thank you.

PRIEST: But I understand, I understand. I place myself in your ... physical ... position, let's say. I put myself in your fiancé's place also. I've already told you that I entered the Church after twenty years in the world, and thank God I kept myself ... and then there was the gift of vocation, shall we say. So I am able to understand your problem, my child. Think about everything we have said to each other today, and come back whenever you like, or, as I said, to the confessor next to me here. All right?

*Now follow some extracts from other conversations in which the priest maintains a severely uncompromising stand.*

CHURCH OF SANTA MARIA IN VIA, ROME

PRIEST: When you are married, child, you may do this act at once, but otherwise not at all.

PENITENT: No, Father, that's not it. I wanted to know what happens if, once we're married, we find there's no sexual harmony between us.

PRIEST: Certainly there will be.

PENITENT: But it happens to so many couples and then they have to separate.

PRIEST: Frankly, are you both capable of doing this thing or aren't you?

PENITENT: I don't know, we've never tried, so I don't know. I'm afraid he'll go with other women.

PRIEST: Why should he?

PENITENT: Because he says he has physiological needs.

PRIEST: This thing must not be done, that's all there is to it.

PENITENT: Excuse me, Father, but you tell me that my marriage will be perfect, from the sexual point of view too, even if I don't have direct proof of it beforehand. You assume this responsibility, in all conscience, of advising me not to try first?

PRIEST: No, it can't happen that there are such things. If there weren't this ... obligation, nobody would be pure when they married.

## SALERNO CATHEDRAL

PENITENT: Listen, Father, my girl friend and I agree perfectly that we want to have full intercourse before marriage, but we're good practicing Catholics—you understand?

PRIEST: And why do you wish to do something that is forbidden by Christ's doctrine? What is there that is more important than God's law that induces you to make this experiment? You're giving me the same argument as a person who says, "I want to avoid paying taxes but I'm a good citizen." Don't you see the contradiction?

PENITENT: Father, you're comparing a crime like tax evasion with a simple wish on our part to acquire a valid and total experience before marriage, which is, according to the Catholic faith, indissoluble and therefore a step which doesn't allow mistakes.

PRIEST: But, my son, tax evasion is a crime against man's law. A sexual relationship outside marriage is a crime against God's law. So the comparison is just.

PENITENT: But, Father, is it conceivable that a man can be asked to remain chaste until he marries, that is, on an average, until he's thirty? According to medical research this would bring about a weakening of the sexual organs and, in some cases, even impotence.

PRIEST: There can be other outlets.

PENITENT: Such as?

PRIEST: Have you ever masturbated?

PENITENT: No, Father. Why would that be preferable? Does a person who masturbates sin less than one who has intercourse with his fiancé?

PRIEST: In a certain sense it's not as grave a sin, because it doesn't involve other people.

CHURCH OF SAN GIOVANNI BATTISTA, IMPERIA

PRIEST: You and your boy friend have been doing some lovemaking? You've gone a bit too far, perhaps? You've done things that are too intimate sometimes?

PENITENT: Yes, that's it, I . . . I don't know.

PRIEST: Speak in a whisper.

PENITENT: I don't know, you see, what I'm allowed to do and what not. Up to what point.

PRIEST: A few kisses, a few caresses, where it's permitted.

PENITENT: That's it, where is it permitted?

PRIEST: It's understood that there are certain parts of the body that must not be caressed when you're engaged but only when you're married, when you will be free to do other things, much more. At present, be content with a few kisses, a few caresses, that's all.

PENITENT: Kisses on the cheek? But a kiss between engaged people is different, isn't it?

PRIEST: But not on the mouth, my child, no—speak quietly, speak quietly—those are the kisses that arouse passions, that can provoke the senses, that can also be troubling.

PENITENT: But between two normal people, what harm is there?

PRIEST: And don't prolong those embraces. You understand what I mean, don't you?

PENITENT: But I don't know—

PRIEST: Prudence, one must be prudent.

PENITENT: But if he wants to do other things, mustn't I let him?

PRIEST: No. To be touched and caressed in other places, delicate places, no. You understand, don't you?

CHURCH OF SANTA MARIA MAGGIORE, TRENT

PRIEST: You surely don't wish to engage in premarital experiments, my daughter?

PENITENT: Why not? After all, proper harmony between two people is necessary, isn't it?

PRIEST: Sexual experiments?

PENITENT: Yes, as well, of course.

PRIEST: Well, listen, there are God's laws—

PENITENT: What laws? God made us in a certain way so that—

PRIEST: Yes, but these relationships are bound up with the family, within which they become legitimate.

PENITENT: All right, but we are two people who love each other and will, therefore, form a family.

PRIEST: But, in the meantime, God bless you, you haven't formed it. That's the first thing, eh? Then, until such time as you have this family, these relations are not possible.

PENITENT: I think it's a natural law that when two people love each other, they should do certain things.

PRIEST: God constituted natural law very definitely upon the family, that's the thing.

PENITENT: All right, but we ought to have some experience first to know each other better. So many marriages fail for the very reason that husbands and wives don't get on sexually.

PRIEST: Let's not exaggerate. But, anyway, if there are any doubts about this point, go to a doctor and be examined.

PENITENT: But a woman can have certain reactions with one man and not with another. The doctor can only find out if there's some physical impediment, but not if there are impediments of a psychological nature.

PRIEST: I agree as to that, but you understand that you cannot go against God's laws to engage in an experiment of that kind.

PENITENT: But why "against God's laws"? That's what I don't understand!

PRIEST: You are going against God's laws because you seek a pleasure that should, rather, be bound up with the conception of children.

## CONCILIATORY PRIESTS

*We have already stated that fourteen priests out of a hundred showed themselves to be readier to engage in a less dogmatic dialogue with the penitent. The most broad-minded and, basically, the most positive, is certainly the one recorded in Rome, at the Church of Sacro Cuore del Suffragio, which is here reported in full.*

CHURCH OF THE SACRO CUORE DEL SUFFRAGIO, ROME

PRIEST: Jesus Christ be prasied.
PENITENT: May He always be praised.
PRIEST: When was your last confession?
PENITENT: Three months ago, I think.
PRIEST: What have you to confess since then?
PENITENT: I don't know, Father. You ask me some questions.
PRIEST: Mass during that time?
PENITENT: Yes, yes, I always go to mass.
PRIEST: Thoughts about God, prayers?
PENITENT: Oh, yes, I believe I say them every morning.
PRIEST: To *say* prayers is always a little less than praying. One's thoughts should always turn to God during the course of the day. Are you sufficiently thoughtful and charitable toward others?
PENITENT: Yes. The thing is that I have a problem I'd like to have your opinion on. I'm engaged and I'm a bit worried about my fiancé. I don't know whether you can understand what I'm saying. There are some physical needs that I'm not able to

repress, so I don't know whether it would be a good thing to have intercourse with him or whether it's better to do it by oneself, that's the thing.

PRIEST: Are you talking about yourself or about him?

PENITENT: The problem is the same for both of us.

PRIEST: We have to be careful not to see needs where there really are none. Certainly, if this affection is not kept upon a serene, healthy plane, there can be something that, leading to a state of uneasiness, excitement, makes it harder to love each other in a serene way, like engaged people and not like married people. But you must see that there is also the possibility of keeping this affection on a more controlled level.

PENITENT: We try. But now, we've arrived at a certain point.

PRIEST: Look, at a certain point, just because of this need for faith, a person has to realize that a certain control is necessary. This is inevitable, otherwise we wouldn't be admitting that there's any difference—apart from other reasons and more elevated motivations—between an engaged couple in love with each other, and a married couple.

PENITENT: Yes, all right, but there's another problem—I mean, the physical one. I've noticed that as a result of controlling ourselves, we feel bad afterward, and so now I don't know whether it's better—

PRIEST: But, you see, it's like a child left with a box of chocolates or a package of sugar within reach. One suffers, it's logical. Often it is just that one does not control oneself enough, does not keep within specific limits in the expression of this affection and that, in this greater freedom, one arrives at an excitement, a disturbance, something that is difficult to control.

PENITENT: Well, that's the situation I am already in, so what I mean is if I seek satisfaction by myself, so as not to go all the way with him . . . I mean, which of the two things is best?

PRIEST: But that's as if you said to me is it better for me to punch or to slap that person? I would suggest that we look at the thing in another way. Let's see if we can avoid both the punch and the slap. In the sense that the excitement that leads to this danger is probably the mark of affectionate behavior that's pushed too far, in its symptoms and in its expressions. You wonder if it is better to satisfy him or to masturbate? I think that the discussion should be in different terms, namely that this affectionate behavior ought not to lead to—

PENITENT: But, you know, it's no longer possible. We aren't two children.

PRIEST: You can't talk about impossibility, because no one believes in impossibility.

PENITENT: I've been thinking that to have normal relations is more natural, isn't it?

PRIEST: Well, yes, objectively speaking, it is more natural. That's logical. But to say that a thing is natural is not the same as saying that it's right.

PENITENT: Nowadays, all engaged couples do it. I don't see why I should go on . . .

PRIEST: You know, it's very primitive for a Christian to say "Everyone does it."

PENITENT: I mean, I think it's important, too, to get to know each other sexually before marrying, isn't it?

PRIEST: I don't know.

PENITENT: I mean, so many marriages break up because of sexual incompatibility.

PRIEST: Yes, yes. But far more engagements break up because of sexual experimentation.

PENITENT: But, Father, isn't it better to break up before marriage, to find out about the incompatibility beforehand, rather than have to live with it for the rest of one's life, irrevocably tied together?

PRIEST: I'm not talking about engaged couples who have shown sexual incompatibility, I'm talking about engagements that have been spoiled at a certain point by sexual intercourse.

PENITENT: Oh, well, then, it wasn't real love. In my opinion it's very clear that if a couple splits up, it obviously means there's something wrong between them. And it's better for this to happen before marriage rather than after.

PRIEST: That's a bit hasty. I think there's another alternative—a feeling might have existed that, at a certain point, was spoiled.

PENITENT: Oh, no, Father, an intelligent person can't spoil a feeling, as you call it, by an act in which he or she participates deliberately. And, anyway, why should the sexual act spoil feelings during an engagement and not during a marriage? The feeling, after all, is made deeper by the physical act, as long as there aren't any sexual incompatibilities.

PRIEST: If the physical act is not a full expression of affection that springs from a whole set of circumstances, it can produce some upsets. In lovemaking a person can't control himself or herself. When this is comforted by affection, it's all right, otherwise all [sexual experiences] are more or less substitutes for love. And you understand, of course, that when these substitutes are given excessive importance, one imagines oneself in love. Otherwise we should have to say that the ideal engagement is one that flowers through sexual experience. And that's doubtful.

PENITENT: But I think, instead, that sexual experience between two people who are going to spend all their lives together is necessary.

PRIEST: Without, however, gaining sexual knowledge through sexual intimacy.

PENITENT: But that's the only way, Father, that one can understand whether one person gets on sexually with the other or not.

PRIEST: It is true, unfortunately, that unexpected things can happen. But I think that two engaged people can very easily, through healthy affectionate actions that can be—

PENITENT: Yes, but when one's in bed, Father, it's different, you can't deny that, and then there are certain reactions that may be—

PRIEST: Now I speak as a man, and not as a priest. I am

supposed to believe that when an engaged man gives way to passion, he does so because of real love. And to give way because of love means being truly desirous of the other person's well-being.

PENITENT: Usually, human love is never ideal. How can one tell whether it's real love? In my opinion, the main thing is for a person to be convinced of it. And if he or she is wrong, they've made a mistake, but in good faith.

PRIEST: Yes, but that seems like oversimplifying things a bit. I've learned from an unfortunately long ministerial experience ... I say long because life in this field almost never brings up anything new ... that it's rather unlikely if, at the moment in which two people arrive at the sexual act, the impulse is that of love properly understood. There is always a moment of surrender, which is weakness, which is passion.

PENITENT: All right, but these are the things of which love is made.

PRIEST: Be that as it may, I don't believe that engaged couples, in the majority of cases, are in a condition to be able to learn from their sexual experiences. How many people, had they a more controlled conjugal life, would know each other less but would be more aware, more conscious of their will power?

PENITENT: Well, what am I supposed to do?

PRIEST: You must try to remain as you are, or try to hurry up the marriage as much as possible. Since, having arrived at this point, it seems to me, all other considerations apart, that everything is there for entering into this final step with serenity, with tranquillity. But if circumstances do not permit the hastening of the marriage, try, at least as far as you can, not to let yourselves get into a situation where you *have* to marry. Because it's a fact that if a person leans too far out of a window and lets himself go, he'll end up on the ground. But I believe you can avoid falling to the ground just by not leaning out too far.

PENITENT: All right.

PRIEST: Remember that when we can say to ourselves—because conscience is of very great importance in the evaluation of these things—that we have done our best, and to do our best doesn't mean that one never makes any mistakes. God understands us and helps us. The important thing is not to resign oneself to making a mistake, do you see? We must not surrender to error.

PENITENT: All right, Father.

PRIEST: As penance we will say an Our Father to Our Lord and a Hail Mary to Our Lady.

*We now reproduce the most interesting extracts from conversations with other conciliatory priests.*

COMO CATHEDRAL

PRIEST: You see, in all conscience I can't say to you that you are or aren't committing a sin. Do you understand? All I say is try to act so that your manifestations of love and your love for this young man are not purely material attitudes. Do you understand? Why did you come to confession, today especially?

PENITENT: Well, because I took my courage in my hands.

PRIEST: It isn't that you've tried to obtain absolution and other priests have refused it?

PENITENT: No, no, I stopped going to confession because some priests went so far as to say that it was a sin to exchange kisses.

PRIEST: What did I tell you? I'm not of that opinion. Anyway, the advice that I can give you is to try and behave during this engagement period and to confess more often, bringing your fiancé as well, maybe. You can pray together in church, go to mass together on Sundays, receive the sacraments together. In this way you can try to be united, seeking agreement not only on the physical level but also on the spiritual and human level, do you understand? And then, you're not made of stone, are you?

Some manifestations of love are necessary to strengthen that affection and love which you both feel for each other as you quite rightly say. Do you understand? All right.

PENITENT: Yes.

## CHURCH OF SAN SIRO, SAN REMO

PENITENT: In short, I want to know how far I can go, in relations with my fiancée, without committing a sin.

PRIEST: You must try not to get into a situation of excitement that will, later, push you into the complete act which is permitted only in marriage.

PENITENT: That is, kisses, caresses, embraces. But you tell me, Father, that when one loves, it becomes inevitable between two normal people that these manifestations of affection turn to desire.

PRIEST: I understand. But just because of this you must be guided by conscience not to go beyond those limits where you are no longer able to control yourself.

PENITENT: But we're not robots that can be turned off by a switch, Father. Also because, if I may say so, intelligence, I mean self-control comes into it. It's easy to exercise it, when there's a logical, convincing reason for doing so.

PRIEST: In this case there is such a reason.

PENITENT: You, Father who have a vocation, who are out of touch with life—

PRIEST: That's what you say!

PENITENT: I can think about a logical reason. But for me who doesn't have the vocation and who lives in the midst of life, there isn't any logical explanation. Indeed, there are logical arguments on the other side. One of them is that it's better to experience full intercourse before marriage, seeing that marriage for the Church is indissoluble, rather than afterward, when it's no longer possible to correct any mistakes that have been made. Another, no less important, is that I don't feel physically capable of arriving at the age of twenty-five without having sexual experience. I'd feel as if I were abnormal, don't you see?

PRIEST: Yes, I see. But you love your fiancée?

PENITENT: Certainly.

PRIEST: Don't you think that if you have relations with her, I mean full intercourse, and then decide to leave each other that you leave her with her virginity gone, no longer intact—doesn't that make you think, seeing that you seem to me to be a responsible person?

PENITENT: Sure it makes me think. But, Father, you preach that in life all good is not on one side, and all evil on the other. And so, for my part, I ask if you think it would be better for me and my fiancée to find out that we don't get on, after being married, maybe with one or two children? Without taking into account the fact that nowadays a woman's virginity is no longer an indispensable factor for marriage as it used to be. I mean, a woman who's not a virgin still has a chance of forming a family, while a woman who is separated from her husband no longer has this possibility. Times have changed, Father, and it's a good thing they have.

PRIEST: Yes, times have changed, in some ways for the better, in some for the worse. [Long pause] And, believe me, it's not easy to sit behind the confessional. One can't say to people, "This is God's will." Nowadays, people like yourself, want to know why God demands certain things. There's great confusion among us too, you see. However, I myself, in these cases, advise only one thing—act according to your conscience. If you act according to your conscience and make mistakes, your mistakes will, at least, be forgiven. Do you understand?

## CONCLUSION: NO PREMARITAL INTERCOURSE

The engaged couples put forward two basic arguments in support of their desire to have intercourse. The first is that premarital experiences serve to establish whether the couple is in sexual harmony. The second is that sexual relations make it possible for the couple to satisfy their physiological needs, which are not sinful if they spring from real love.

The stand taken by the priests is unanimous: five minutes before marriage, nothing; five minutes after marriage, everything.

# III

## COMPLETE SEXUAL RELATIONS BETWEEN ENGAGED COUPLES?

THE FOLLOWING series of conversations differs from the previous series in that the engaged couple is already having full sexual intercourse. The basic question being asked here is whether they should consider themselves outside the Church or not.

We recorded 116 conversations. The majority of the priests, faced with the *fait accompli*, were prepared to give absolution if the penitent promised to stop having sex with his fiancée. In only one in eight cases did the priest give absolution even though the penitent plainly intended to continue his or her premarital relations.

### "BREAK OFF ALL SEXUAL RELATIONS IMMEDIATELY"

*Almost all the priests heard—104 out of 116—took a condemnatory stand with engaged couples who have already had full sexual intercourse. Only admission of the error committed and a promise not to repeat it could permit absolution.*

CHURCH OF SAN FRANCESCO, BRESCIA

PRIEST: How long has it been since your last confession?

PENITENT: Several months.

PRIEST: Do you go to mass on Sundays?

PENITENT: Yes.

PRIEST: Regularly?

PENITENT: Yes.

PRIEST: Why have you gone so long without taking communion?

PENITENT: Because I've had a crisis. I'm engaged to a man and I've had intimate relations with him. I was afraid that—

PRIEST: Good, good! You were right to be afraid. [*Long pause*] You know that now you are no longer in the grace of God and that if you die you will be banished to the flames of hell? Do you know that?

PENITENT: The fact is, I'm not convinced about committing a sin. My fiancé and I love each other, we mean to get married, and we want to know if, besides affection, there is also sexual harmony that will ensure a strong marriage bond.

PRIEST: You think you're clever, don't you? Christ gave us laws that have lasted for two thousand years and you, all innocent, come here and blow the whole thing up in two minutes.

PENITENT: I don't think I'm blowing anything up, Father.

PRIEST: Oh, sure, sure. But now, tell me. Are these relations with your fiancé frequent?

PENITENT: Well, I don't know . . . yes.

PRIEST: How many times a week do you make love with him?

PENITENT: I've never thought to count them, Father. What's the importance of the number of times?

PRIEST: But you already know everything, my dear child! According to you, to sin once or to sin ten times is the same thing.

PENITENT: That's not the point. The point is, whether it's a sin or not. The number of times is only of relative importance.

PRIEST: And she insists! That's what you say. A person may give way by mistake, but in that case he or she makes a mistake once or twice, not a thousand times. Now do you understand why I asked you how many times?

PENITENT: But I've explained to you, Father, that it's not a question of making a mistake. We decided to do it consciously in the conviction that it is not a sin. If you say that it is a sin and that I must consider myself outside the Church, I'm sorry because I believe that I'm a good and honest Catholic in every other way, but I won't stop making love with my fiancé for that reason.

PRIEST: And if you get pregnant?

PENITENT: We take precautions.

PRIEST: Oh, fine, it gets better and better—you pile sin upon sin. But, naturally, for you it's convenient to say that the sexual act, without intent of procreation is quite a normal thing, completely normal. Is that right? And, for goodness' sake, what are these precautions of yours?

PENITENT: I don't know, the usual precautions.

PRIEST: Oh, sure the usual precautions. What *are* the usual precautions? Does he, perhaps use prophylactics?

PENITENT: What?

PRIEST: Well . . . condoms.

PENITENT: No.

PRIEST: Well, then, does he withdraw before coming?

PENITENT: Sometimes.

PRIEST: You see! He disperses his seed, the seed that God has given man for procreation. Does that seem right to you? Do you think God can approve of this?

PENITENT: But recently even the Church admitted that the purpose of the sexual act is not always and solely procreation but is also enjoyment of the senses, within the framework of true love.

PRIEST: Let's say within the framework of marriage. [*Pause*] I suppose that you caress his member until he reaches orgasm, and that he does the same with your sex, it's like that, isn't it?

PENITENT: Well . . .

PRIEST: You see that it's not just the desire for knowing each other that urges you toward these . . . things that you call experiences. It's also pleasure as an end in itself. Because these lascivious touchings produce nothing but erotic paroxysms and do not—

PENITENT: But these are normal sexual manifestations, that are suggested nowadays, even by Catholic handbooks.

PRIEST: Yes, but between married people, to preserve physical attraction. Outside marriage, they are grave abandonments because they are eroticism without any purpose, without any justification.

PENITENT: That doesn't seem right to me. They are manifestations of sexuality, but of affection too. Indeed, with my fiancé I do these things willingly. With another person for whom I don't feel anything I'd never do them. And I think, too, that they're necessary, to gauge our harmony on the physical level, before uniting ourselves definitely in marriage.

PRIEST: Mistaken reasoning, my dear!

PENITENT: All right. I've realized, Father, that you don't like me. You treat me as if . . . as if I were the devil in person—

PRIEST: No one could say, with the ideas you've put into your head, that you can be considered a little angel! But I'm not angry with you. Your assuredness about certain things bothers me. You're committing sin and claiming that you're not. Understand? My dear, you can do as you please with your fiancé when and where you like, but you can't claim to do it with heaven's blessing. Understand? Think over what I've said to you. A Christian must be humble, a servant of God. You claim that you can dictate to God, and you want me to respect you. Ah, everything happens to me!

PENITENT: Don't worry, Father, I'm going now. I don't think, though, that you have the humility of a servant of God, as you were saying just now.

PRIEST: All right, all right, let's leave it at that. Obviously I can't give you absolution, but I can give you a blessing. Does that satisfy you?

PENITENT: Thank you, Father.


## CHURCH OF THE DOMINICANS, BOLZANO

PRIEST: Has it been a long time since you confessed?

PENITENT: I don't remember exactly.

PRIEST: A month?

PENITENT: Longer, maybe three?

PRIEST: Is there any special reason why you waited so long?

PENITENT: Well, yes. I don't really want to confess so much as ask your opinion. I've had intimate relations with my fiancée and I thought I wouldn't get absolution from the confessor so—

PRIEST: You're mistaken, my son. I can give you absolution. You see, I'll explain it all to you immediately. Before marriage, God forbids any kind of sexual relationship which is not just a mere demonstration of love, of affection. But the world in which we live, unfortunately, is full of temptations—even for us ministers of Christ—so that a person can slip, make a mistake. The important thing is to realize that one has erred, and to try to put things right immediately. Now, my son, you must make an act of contrition before God, you must promise him, willingly, that you will not do it again. You owe respect to your fiancée, you owe her consideration, you cannot drag her through the mud to satisfy your selfish pleasures. Do you see?

PENITENT: No, let me explain, Father. I'm not convinced of having made a mistake. My fiancée and I entered into these sexual relations willingly, we were both in agreement. We are convinced that before arriving at marriage, and tying ourselves down for good, it's necessary to know each other in every way, including the sexual way, to avoid mistakes that would be irreparable otherwise.

PRIEST: No, it's a very serious error, my son, even if you

have made it in good faith. To mistake an engagement for marriage—what, then, would you find in marriage that's new?

PENITENT: Family, children, problems in common, life together.

PRIEST: Yes, very well, but what you are doing now has been established by God as the first seal of matrimonial life. Think how fine it is to exchange your love in a complete way, after the benediction of God.

PENITENT: Yes, it is fine, but it can also be very dangerous. What if one realizes then that there is sexual incompatibility? What does one do? I have a friend who found himself in this situation. He went to his confessor and told him of his problems. The confessor replied, "Marriage is a serious thing, you ought to have thought about that before. Now, you are tied for the rest of your life, man cannot put apart that which God has joined." You see, Father?

PRIEST: Yes, I see, but it isn't necessary to go as far as premarital relations to know whether there's affinity between two engaged people. All that's needed is a little tact, sensitivity, intelligence.

PENITENT: But I can't see why this blessed sexual act has to be considered a sin. In the past, perhaps it was necessary, because people were ignorant and didn't know enough. But people are more responsible now, they know more. The Church ought to take that into account, shouldn't it?

PRIEST: The Church does what God has told it to do, my son, and God's laws can't keep up with the times. They are universal, immutable.

PENITENT: Yes, but until quite recently the exchange of a mere kiss between engaged people was considered a sin. Now, a limitation of that kind would be laughable.

PRIEST: But that is something marginal, not fundamental like this other thing which involves the essence of the Christian family. God did not say, "Do not kiss each other," but he did say, "Do not join yourselves together before marriage."

PENITENT: Father, I think that's a very hypocritical way of facing problems or, rather, of not facing them, of evading them. Anyway, thanks.

PRIEST: You, my son, are accusing God of hypocrisy, do you know that? When you're a bit . . . when you're my age, you won't think like that any more, I assure you . . . Do you want absolution?

PENITENT: Even if I don't promise anything?

PRIEST: No, you must promise me that you will not fall into errors of that kind any more, my son. You must promise God.

PENITENT: I don't feel I can do that, Father. If I ever do, I'll come back.

PRIEST: All right, my son. In the meantime, pray to God for enlightenment.


CHURCH OF SANTA CROCE AL FLAMINIO, ROME

PRIEST: What have you to confess?

PENITENT: Father, I find myself in a special situation, because I'm having intimate relations with my fiancé. I've tried to reason with him, but, after all, he's right too, from a certain point of view, because he says we have to get to know one another sexually as well, so as not to make an irreparable mistake through marriage.

PRIEST: That's not true.

PENITENT: What's not true?

PRIEST: Because experience has taught me that the continuity of marriage almost never depends on the sexual temperament of the couples. And I do have a certain amount of experience, considering all I've heard in the confessional. If what you say were right, it would mean that pleasure is more important than faith. And this is why faith is in a bad way. Jesus said, "Man, the animal, will never understand that which is spiritual."

PENITENT: But man is made up of spirit and matter, isn't he?

PRIEST: The spirit is superior to matter.

PENITENT: But what if, after marriage, a person realizes that there's no sexual harmony? I know of examples among my women friends. It happens, you know.

PRIEST: You can't consider marriage only from the sexual side.

PENITENT: Not *only* from that side, but *also* from that side.

PRIEST: Yes, of course, but marriage should be considered as a whole and not by sections. You see, sexual harmony is reached after a ripening that can take place only after marriage, and with living together. Of course, there are problems of a purely physiological nature—

PENITENT: That's it!

PRIEST: But they must be subordinated, coordinated with all the rest, because—

PENITENT: In short, am I sinning or not when I have intimate relations with my fiancé?

PRIEST: A girl who experiences, who has these intimate relations . . . it's not right, you understand. There are so many other things to discover in a man, in a fiancé, that will show you whether he will be a perfect husband, whether he likes to work, whether he is of good character—

PENITENT: I agree with that. But if I think that my fiancé, going by these things, will be a perfect husband, and marry him, and then I find out that we don't get on sexually? You priests say that these things are taboo, that sex—

PRIEST: Of course! Priests obtain their teachings from the word of Christ. In giving yourself to your fiancé, you're acting in a reproachful way.

PENITENT: I'm not harming anyone, am I?

PRIEST: There's no need to harm one's neighbor, you're harming yourself. You're transgressing the word of the gospel. Do you think that's all it takes to go to heaven, not to harm anyone?

PENITENT: I don't say that, it's just that it seems to me—

PRIEST: It's not for you to judge. Are you possibly trying to justify your behavior? You must not think of this, if you wish to continue your confession. You have sinned in having intimate relations with your fiancé, all right, but now you must convince yourself that it's not right to do this, and you must promise yourself that you will sin no more. Have you any doubts regarding this?

PENITENT: I understand. But, yes, I do have some doubts.

PRIEST: Very well, if you have some doubts it's not worth continuing the discussion now, you can return sometime when you're calmer. You must reject your fiancé's proposals, you must cut him off short, as they say. You'll have all the time in the world to think about your sexual harmony. For the present, prepare yourself for marriage conscientiously, try to live a tranquil life with mutual respect, *mutual,* he must respect you, and you him.

PENITENT: Yes, but that—

PRIEST: That's all there is to it.

PENITENT: All right, but you know perfectly well that it's necessary to know, otherwise there might be something unexpected.

PRIEST: It is important, but you can find out in other ways.

PENITENT: Find out in what sense?

PRIEST: Well, if there's fear of some illness, of some impossibility, all that's needed is a medical certificate. In some countries it's obligatory.

PENITENT: I won't insist, Father, because you're in a hurry. But I could point out to you that two people may not get on sexually even though they're normal. That's what I mean. There can be selfishness on the man's part, I don't know, other things.

PRIEST: Yes, but you can learn from all those things, if you pay attention, without any need for intimate relations. After all, there are only a few cases in which marriages fail due to sexual incomprehension. Usually it's because one of the partners has shown bad faith by hiding something from the other.

PENITENT: All right, you talk about bad faith when instead it's something more objective.

PRIEST: Very well, let's see. The sin has already been committed, anyway. How did it start?

PENITENT: How did it start? I don't know, we stayed together—

PRIEST: Like husband and wife?

PENITENT: Well, yes.

PRIEST: How many times?

PENITENT: I never counted!

PRIEST: That's bad!

PENITENT: Why? Is it important to count the times? If we've been together once or ten times—does that change the evaluation of the sin?

PRIEST: Yes, because an error, committed once, is more understandable. It could have been due to a momentary loss of control. But a recurrence of the error signifies a desire to err.

PENITENT: Ah!

PRIEST: Well, then, did you stay together once, twice a month?

PENITENT: Nothing regular like that.

PRIEST: Well, roughly, how many times since your last confession?

PENITENT: I don't know, it's six months since I confessed, I don't know.

PRIEST: Ten times or so?

PENITENT: Maybe more, I don't know. But is the exact number of times so important?

PRIEST: Yes, the number of sins committed. You lack the concept of sin.

PENITENT: Maybe. But anyway, under these conditions, can I hope to obtain absolution?

PRIEST: Under these conditions, no. You must meditate, you must arrive at the realization that to give in to your fiancé before marriage is contrary to the teaching of Christ. When you come here and say to me, "I have sinned, I know that I have sinned, I will sin no more," I will give you absolution. All right?

PENITENT: All right. Thank you.

## CHURCH OF SAN LORENZO, FLORENCE

PRIEST: What sins have you committed?

PENITENT: The most serious sin is that I'm engaged to a man and I've had intimate relations with him. Naturally, this means a continuous struggle for me.

PRIEST: Do you go to mass on Sundays?

PENITENT: Yes.

PRIEST: Do you behave well at work? Where do you work?

PENITENT: I'm an office worker.

PRIEST: In your relationships with others, with your colleagues and friends, do you try to behave well, in a Christian way, in your way of speaking and acting?

PENITENT: Yes, of course, I try to be. But this relationship with my fiancé bothers me, it—

PRIEST: That's a situation which, once you've created it, is hard to get rid of, because you have to be able to convince yourself, little by little, that love does not consist in doing these things. Real love will be that which comes when you're married. For the moment it's not—

PENITENT: Yes, I know, but I've agreed to do it. *Sometimes* I've agreed. What do you advise me to do?

PRIEST: I would advise you to do things with conviction, rather than breaking things off hastily. To break things off hastily can lead to unpleasant situations. On the other hand, doing things according to a certain criterion, exercising pressure on your fiancé to convince him, to—

PENITENT: No. He's already told me that these premarital experiences are necessary, in order to avoid—

PRIEST: Are necessary? If he has genital organs and you have genital organs, there's no need for these experiences. Why, are you afraid that once you're married you'll no longer be capable of doing it? In fact, as a result of these very experiences, once married, you might easily find that you'll no longer be capable, just as, once married, you may very possibly not have any children.

PENITENT: Oh, no! It may be that . . . but if we don't get on, sexually?

PRIEST: Those are all things that people say to suit their own convenience. Because if you were to say no to him, wouldn't he be capable of stopping there?

PENITENT: No, we've discussed this lots of times, naturally.

PRIEST: And what does he say to that?

PENITENT: He says that if two people love each other, these things are natural.

PRIEST: Natural, yes, but they must be complete. You have to go on until you become pregnant. Then things are complete. But to break them off is not natural.

PENITENT: You mean that if relations are not complete—

PRIEST: A complete relationship is necessary.

PENITENT: All right, but that's a sin, according to the Church, isn't it?

PRIEST: Yes, but between husband and wife it's not a sin because adultery, fornication, are things against nature.

PENITENT: How against nature, Father?

PRIEST: Listen, I have to say my office, the choir has already begun. If we go on talking here— Outside marriage these things are not lawful because you don't do the whole thing. To be a natural and complete thing, it has to arrive at procreation.

PENITENT: Well, then, if we do the complete act I could get pregnant.

PRIEST: That's your own affair. Don't do it, you know it's a dangerous game, don't do it. What am I to say to you? I can tell you that outside marriage this thing is not lawful, since you don't arrive at the true aim of sexual union at the true purpose.

PENITENT: So, then—

PRIEST: It doesn't mean that you deny your mutual love. These are rather delicate things that should never be allowed to begin, and if begun, you must try to do things in the best possible way, by conviction. If you really do love one another, there's no need to say this.

PENITENT: All right, but I can't take Communion, I mean, I can't confess, can I?

PRIEST: To confess oneself, one confesses—

PENITENT: No, I mean if I go on just the same would you give me absolution?

PRIEST: Listen, if you put in so many "ifs" and "buts," we'll never get to the point.

PENITENT: In order to get absolution I have to promise not to do it any more, don't I?

PRIEST: If it were up to you alone, would you continue to do it?

PENITENT: Well, I love him so, I mean, I like it too, really. I'm not making any sacrifice. But, since my conscience—

PRIEST: Look, before midnight I've got to say my office, which I've missed on your account. This is the important thing. Before God we take things as we know them without arguing too much, we place ourselves as we feel in our conscience before God. We try to do our best, Our Lord doesn't ask us to do the impossible. What am I to say to you? If the moralists had been married, they wouldn't have written so many restrictions on morality. You do as you think best, try to improve yourself. It's not that we, when we come to confess, say the things that those cursed nuns have taught us. I'd cut off all their heads rather than call them daughters of Christ. Cursed nuns, I call them because they say, "We don't intend doing it again," rather than counseling improvement. Because not doing it any more is for children: "Don't you do it any more!" [imitating a child's voice] And a few minutes later, they've done it once more. Let's try, rather, to improve ourselves in some way, to improve our situation. I told you at the start, you won't be able to stop all of a sudden. Try to get on the right road and little by little you'll manage to do something. This is the criterion for improving our spiritual life. Because, after confession, we have the same feelings, the same strength. Let's try to improve, to do it less often. Only thus will we manage to do better. This is the criterion of confession. All right? On the basis of this criterion, I can give absolution. But you must say to me, "Look, I can't say I won't do it any more, and therefore I can't receive absolution. I will try to improve, in some way at least, to make it just a little more acceptable."

PENITENT: A resolution.

PRIEST: A resolution to improve is hardly a resolution not to commit sin again. If it depended on us alone, well, yes, but it doesn't depend on us alone, the resolution to improve in something, eh?

PENITENT: Yes.

PRIEST: Anyway, ask God's forgiveness for everything you remember or don't know in your past life, and try to have the will power to do your best to live always in gladness with the Lord, eh?

*The most interesting extracts from other conversations based on this type of situation follow; in them the priests maintained uncompromising stands.*

CHURCH OF ST. AGOSTINO, SALERNO

PENITENT: The fact that I have intercourse with my girl friend, Father, doesn't mean that I'm taking advantage of her, but that I have a valid relationship with her, both emotionally and sexually.

PRIEST: You're taking advantage of her all the same, because even if women have equal rights with men they're still physiologically handicapped. Your girl friend will bear the mark of her affair with you, whereas you'll be the same as before.

PENITENT: Father, I can't accept this reasoning. It reduces virginity to a question of a membrane being intact. I believe that virginity is something different, nothing to do with whether one has had sexual intercourse or not. Virginity, in my opinion, is in the awareness that you give yourself to someone for love, not purely and simply out of desire. You give yourself with the knowledge of doing so within a valid relationship. In this sense I see men and women as being equal.

PRIEST: These are a lot of fine words, my dear young man, but in practice? Would you marry a girl who had already belonged to someone else?

PENITENT: Yes, if I knew it had been a serious relationship and not just a caprice. Why shouldn't I?

PRIEST: As long as you're content. However, apart from all this, there still remains the fact of God's law. God established the sacramental nature of marriage in order to give Christian legitimacy to the sexual act and procreation. If you won't accept this rule, you're rejecting practically the whole of Christian teaching. No one can oblige you to follow it—it all depends on your conscience.

PENITENT: Very well, but even if all this is accepted, do you seriously believe that a man can reach thirty, the average age for marriage, without having had sexual intercourse?

PRIEST: But there's no need to have it with your fiancée, your future bride.

PENITENT: And with whom, then?

PRIEST: Don't play innocent, you know perfectly well with whom.

PENITENT: With prostitutes?

PRIEST: For a start, it's a question of commitment and, with God's help, praying to him, thinking of him, one can even manage to maintain one's chastity. And then, if one really can't do without it's certainly much better to sin with a mercenary woman than to offend one's own woman.

PENITENT: If I've understood you correctly, you maintain that a bestial outlet with a prostitute is less sinful than the willing and affectionate relationship I have with my fiancée?

PRIEST: I don't maintain any such thing. I say that Jesus recommended chastity and you say you cannot manage this.

PENITENT: I didn't say that. I said that I think premarital chastity is absurd for many reasons, among them the fact that it's better to know each other sexually before marriage rather than afterward, and also because frustrations of a sexual nature and various mortifications of natural instincts seem to me to be harmful and out of place.

PRIEST: You are trying to confuse me with arguments that ... Only one thing is certain for a Christian—God's law. And God's law speaks plainly: full sexual relations are allowed only after the sacrament of marriage. All the rest is mere academic discussion, which I refuse to continue.

CHURCH OF THE SANTISSIMA ANNUNZIATA, GENOA

PENITENT: You see, I'm engaged and my fiancé ... we don't hold ourselves back, we have intimate relations.

PRIEST: And when are you getting married?

PENITENT: Next year, maybe. You see, at this point I don't know how much I can allow him to do. I know all my women friends have normal intimate relations.

PRIEST: Look, for a Christian, it doesn't matter whether or not the majority fails in its duties. Basically, you ask, what can I allow him to do?

PENITENT: But it's different—

PRIEST: Yes, it's different, but you mustn't allow any more. Some kisses, but in greeting, of affection, that's all.

PENITENT: In greeting?

PRIEST: Yes.

PENITENT: A kiss between engaged people isn't like a kiss between brother and sister, is it?

PRIEST: It ought to be, under such conditions.

PENITENT: But it's absurd, it's unnatural.

PRIEST: How unnatural? I consider kissing an expression of affection.

PENITENT: It is. But there's affection and affection. That is, unless you claim that the affection between brother and sister is the same as between a woman and a man who are engaged.

PRIEST: But, you see, there are all sorts of things in this world, all sorts of things. It all depends what line a person takes. There are lovers, aren't there? And streetwalkers? And adulterers? There's everything. And you. It all depends what category you want to be in.

PENITENT: But I'm a normal person, living normally and so—

PRIEST: There's everything. Pardon me, but I don't understand. Why do you want to stop halfway?

PENITENT: I don't understand.

PRIEST: You say that your friends have intimate relations, don't you?

PENITENT: Yes.

PRIEST: Well, then. Is that a natural thing, according to you?

PENITENT: I think it's right to be able to find out about sexual matters. After all, there are cases of separation and divorce. I'd like to avoid making these mistakes. It's better to make a mistake before, when there's still time to correct it, isn't it?

PRIEST: You're making a mistake even before you start. You give your body to someone who does not yet have any right to it. For a Christian, only the sacrament of marriage gives both parties the right to dispose of their bodies and everything connected with it. You give yours beforehand and you think it's all right? Do as you please! What do I care? I have to expound the thought of Christ and that's all. Then, you can do whatever you like. You're free, aren't you? But I ask if you have a conscience or not. You talk about natural things, but these are supernatural things. You justify everything in this way.

PENITENT: Then I want to know what is allowed before marriage.

PRIEST: What's allowed? Sensuality is not allowed, so there.

PENITENT: But then it would be wrong to go with each other. Because when we're together, there must be some form of physical attraction, mustn't there?

PRIEST: Oh, yes. But all love must be in conformity with God's laws. A mother has immense love for her children—

PENITENT: But it's a different kind of love, Father!

PRIEST: No. You and your man ought to have a love like that between a mother and her children, instead of what you want. You have turned it into the kind of love that exists between married people.


CHURCH OF SAN BIAGIO NEL CARMINE, MODENA

PRIEST: You say you want some advice, my son, but if you have already had marital relations with your fiancée, what advice do you want me to give you?

PENITENT: I wanted to know, Father, if because of this, because of having intercourse with my fiancée, I have to consider myself outside the Church or not.

PRIEST: I wouldn't say that, but you're no longer in the grace of God, you have denied the divine precepts, yes. You're outside, but if you repent and decide to return to an observance of the laws of God, the Church will welcome you with open arms, you see.

PENITENT: Still, Father, I'd like you to explain to me why I lose the grace of God if I have intimate relations with my girl friend. It's the Church that maintains that matrimony is a serious thing for which one must prepare conscientiously and with full commitment. It's the Church that establishes that marriage is indissoluble, so that any mistake one makes becomes a final mistake. Therefore, I can't understand why the Church itself considers immoral those sexual relations between engaged people that are fundamental, along with many other things, in establishing whether there is complete harmony between two people that can last through the years. I've seen precise and scientific statistics. At least fifteen marriages out of a hundred fail within the first four years due to sexual dissatisfaction on the part of one of the partners.

PRIEST: Calm down! Why are you holding a meeting? But, even if you are right, you're addressing the wrong person. It's not to me that you must address this speech but to God. I'm the spokesman for God's laws and, here in the confessional, I can only repeat that when you behave this way, you disobey those laws. And then I can only say, do whatever your conscience dictates.

PENITENT: I understand. You wash your hands of it. You say, "This is the law, either obey it or go your own way." But does that seem fair to you? Apart from the fact that there are numerous Catholic theologians who contest the divine nature of these rulings, apart from the fact that some of these rulings have altered due to force of circumstances, I was asking whether you, in conscience, can condemn two young people who have a responsible, loving, and complete relationship between them in order to arrive at marriage better prepared, or to break off the relationship before marriage should it prove to be inharmonious and doomed to failure. This is what I wanted to ask you, Father, with humility and without the slightest intention of holding a meeting.

PRIEST: And I've already answered you. In conscience, I can't help but condemn you because the Church, spokesman for the laws of God, does not admit complete sexual relationship, except in marriage. If I thought otherwise, I, too, would have to leave the Church, do you understand? I don't say that your observations are right or wrong. I merely say that they do not fit in with those of the Catholic Church, that's all. So, you must draw the necessary conclusions.

CHURCH OF GESU E MARIA AL CORSO, ROME

PENITENT: My problem is that I have intimate relations with my fiancé.

PRIEST: I see. Now will you allow me to ask you some questions?

PENITENT: Yes, of course.

PRIEST: How do you view the engagement period?

PENITENT: It's for getting to know each other before getting married, before living together. I mean getting to know each other in all ways, from the sexual point of view as well, so as to avoid mistakes in the future. I feel that this mutual confidence and knowledge is important for the formation of a healthy family in the future. Otherwise, there's the danger of separation, of divorce.

PRIEST: Well, look, your motive is all right. Yes, your ideal, your viewpoint is the very central theme of the engagement period. Are we agreed to this?

PENITENT: Yes.

PRIEST: But, the problem is the way in which you intend to arrive at this mutual knowledge. Mutual knowledge, understood as full knowledge, yes, but, after all, there's no need for premarital experience to gain this full knowledge.

PENITENT: What do you mean? Marriage is important—

PRIEST: Yes, most important. But certain things are, in themselves—how shall I say?—forbidden, condemned. Not condemned, however, because of manners, because one day some pope said, "This must not be done." No, there is a divine law which says, "Do not commit impure acts—fornication."

PENITENT: I don't understand why these things are considered impure acts.

PRIEST: Well, they are. If they weren't, what would be the difference between the married state and the unmarried state?

PENITENT: During engagement, a person can find out that he

or she has made a mistake and turn back. This seems to me an important thing.

PRIEST: Yes, it is important, but engagement is still not marriage. It is only within marriage that one may procreate.

PENITENT: But we're not procreating.

PRIEST: Yes, but every sexual act must be carried through to completion, because if one performs an incomplete sexual act—that is, if one performs the sexual act in such a way that there is no possibility of having children—

PENITENT: And if one does this?

PRIEST: It's not allowed.

PENITENT: It may not have been allowed in the past, but I think it is now.

PRIEST: No, no. And why should it be allowed now?

PENITENT: So many of the Church's laws have changed, and it seems to me that this one has, too.

PRIEST: No, not this one, certainly not.


## YES TO PREMARITAL INTERCOURSE
## BETWEEN ENGAGED COUPLES

*As we have said, 116 conversations were recorded concerning the typical situation of a betrothed couple engaging in full sexual intercourse with each other. In 104 cases, the attitude of the priest was uncompromising, as we have just seen. In eight cases, the priest granted absolution in spite of the fact that the penitent claimed that he or she did not wish to end premarital relations.*


CHURCH OF SAN PIETRO E PAOLO, PESCASSEROLI

PRIEST: How long is it since your last confession?

PENITENT: Several months, I don't know.

PRIEST: Not even at Easter?

PENITENT: No, not then, either.

PRIEST: What have you done wrong?

PENITENT: I don't know, Father, I'd like you to question me.

PRIEST: Well, have you committed sins in speaking? Some imprecation? Some gossiping about other people's affairs? Some lies?

PENITENT: No, no.

PRIEST: Have you been to mass, madam?

PENITENT: Of course.

PRIEST: And have you taken Communion?

PENITENT: No, I haven't confessed.

PRIEST: But it's not sin not to confess, if there has been no mortal sin. Is there, perhaps, some sinful relationship?

PENITENT: Well, yes. I have intimate relations with my fiancé.

PRIEST: You're not married?

PENITENT: No.

PRIEST: Well, all right, but then we must talk in private. Let's do this. We don't have time to talk about these things now, do we? Well, then, when mass is ended, when there's more time, why don't we have a little talk, eh?

PENITENT: But I meant . . . since I came to get some advice—

PRIEST: Very well, but you see I can't tell you anything because that one down there is in charge of internal discipline . . . you understand how I'm placed, don't you? Now, when mass is over, we'll have a little talk on our own. What do you say to that?

PENITENT: All right. We'll see.

PRIEST: Fine, now you go and take Communion. I don't know whether the one who was here before allowed you to take it.

PENITENT: How's that? I didn't understand what you said.

PRIEST: Communion, if the confessor that was here before let you take it?

PENITENT: Er, no. It's been a long time since I took it.

PRIEST: Well, then, this is what we'll do. You do it in private, see? Do you agree?

PENITENT: Confess in private?

PRIEST: No, no, Communion. I'll say it for you. Do you agree?

PENITENT: All right.

PRIEST: Go and take Communion now, and when mass is over, go into the sacristy without letting anyone see. Then we can talk comfortably, eh? We'll have a little chat together. All right, young lady? And I'll be at your disposal, because these are things that can be adjusted. Nothing else, young lady?

PENITENT: No.

PRIEST: Say three Hail Marys to Our Lady. Act of Contrition.


CHURCH OF SANT 'ALESSIO, ROME

PRIEST: May Jesus Christ be praised.

PENITENT: May He always be praised.

PRIEST: How long is it since you last confessed?

PENITENT: A long time—four or five months.

PRIEST: What sins have you committed in the meantime?

PENITENT: Well, Father, I came for some advice rather than to confess myself. The fact is that I'm engaged to a girl and I have intimate relations with her. The last time I confessed, the priest said I couldn't receive absolution and so—

PRIEST: It isn't as simple as that.

PENITENT: But—

PRIEST: I mean that one can't liquidate this problem super-ficially, limiting oneself to issuing a sentence of absolution or nonabsolution. The confessor is not a judge but a confidant, and as such he must know how to penetrate into the heart of the penitent so as to get beyond the sin.

PENITENT: That's what I'm looking for, to be understood, to—

PRIEST: Let's see now. Why do you have intimate relations with your fiancée?

PENITENT: There are various reasons. The first is that both of us feel it's necessary, before taking the final step of marriage, to have full mutual knowledge, and full knowledge cannot exclude the sexual side, which, after all, always has considerable importance in married life. Then, because we love each other, we are young, and our demonstrations of affection tend to wind up, instinctively, in intercourse. We don't see any valid reason for setting limits, for frustrating ourselves with renunciations which could result in harming us.

PRIEST: Have you given due thought to the consequences if you were to leave each other later?

PENITENT: Yes, we discussed this before we stayed together for the first time. But we decided that it would be better to leave each other before marriage if we realized that we weren't made for each other, rather than find ourselves with a broken marriage later.

PRIEST: I see that you have very clear ideas and a certain sense of responsibility. As a priest, I cannot approve this attitude of yours, but I can find justification for it. I can understand it, and I can also accept it.

PENITENT: But how is it that you say these things to me, while other confessors condemn these situations at once and without any possibility of appeal?

PRIEST: I too, as I told you, condemn these situations because they are dangerous situations which often do more harm than good. But, you see, there are exceptions, exceptions that are getting more numerous as time goes on. You have spoken to me with a sense of responsibility about your situation, and you have allowed me to understand that you would never use the freedom you have taken to do harm.

PENITENT: No, certainly not.

PRIEST: Good. You see, I am convinced that the laws, the strictures laid down by the Church, were most useful in the days when man's ignorance would have trampled upon any freedom that was granted, making use of it in the worst possible way. Today, they must be understood in a less rigid manner. I would condemn you without the slightest hesitation if you had physical relations with your girl friend that were an end in themselves, but I don't feel that I can condemn you if the physical relations between you take place as the culminating act of affection, of love, of sincere integration. From this point of view there is no difference, toward God, between you and two people who are legally married. You exchange the same sort of affection and you intend to consolidate this affection, later, through the statement of matrimony.

PENITENT: I understand.

PRIEST: I think that in these cases only conscience can be your guide. If a person acts in peace with his conscience, he may be assured that God is with him. When, on the other hand, a person goes against his conscience, this means that something is wrong, that we are moving away from God.

PENITENT: Can I have absolution, then?

PRIEST: Yes, I can give you absolution. I know that other confessors wouldn't give it to you, but consider my act as that of confidence in your sense of responsibility. It would be dangerous for the Church to say, officially, that it was leaving the way free for premarital relations. There are still far too many irresponsible people, incapable of healthy self-control.

PENITENT: I think you, Father, for your confidence.

PRIEST: Have you other things to confess?

PENITENT: No, I don't remember any.

PRIEST: Well, say three Our Fathers, three Hail Marys and three Glorias to Our Lady for penance. Now, recite the Act of Contrition.

CHURCH OF SANT 'ALESSIO, ROME

PENITENT: Father, it's a very long time since I've confessed. I've come here today, perhaps because I feel guilty. You see, I am engaged to a man and I've had intimate relations with him, naturally. I don't know, maybe it's a sin, maybe these things are natural, I don't know. What do you say?

PRIEST: The first relations with one's fiancé are, certainly, a transition from friendship to love. These relations, as time goes on, can become more intense, outwardly, but they must always remain within certain specific limits, partly because we must reserve the joy of total gift for marriage, and partly for various other reasons.

PENITENT: But, you understand that two people who love each other . . . We did try at first, of course, until we were sure that it was serious. After all, we're not doing any harm to anyone. Why does the Church say that it's a sin? That's what I want to know.

PRIEST: Well, you know that total giving of yourself is made only when there is security. Engagement is only a promise which has no legal value.

PENITENT: But, you see, if we get married and then don't get along sexually, which is most important in marriage, then it's a disaster. But if we find out before, we can avoid making a mistake.

PRIEST: This is a real problem, undoubtedly. However, it's necessary to see whether one must go all the way or not in order to get to know one another, to see how you get along in intimate relations.

PENITENT: Well, how far can one go?

PRIEST: It's difficult to say. I'd say this, that first of all you must try to love one another truly, with your hearts and souls. This, certainly, is the thing that God loves best. Then, of course, you can also express your love. I would say that, as things go on, seeing that you have already been engaged for some time, there will be increasing familiarity, let's say physical, between you, which is a natural thing. There are certain acts that one performs in intimacy which you know about, and if you allow yourself to be led into them it's up to your own conscience. I am a priest and therefore know nothing of such things, so we give advice, as we can, within the limits of what we read, of what people tell us. Well, I'd say this, that when you see that certain acts are so intimate that they will necessarily lead to a total union, you ought to try to avoid these intimate acts, and control them. This is always possible if the will is there, since you realize that you are only engaged, and not married, don't you? So there is a certain difference. Try to be good, for your own sakes, and also to avoid awkwardness. If, then, carried away by your affection, you go too far and fall into sin like many another, at least you realize that you have made a mistake. It may very well be that God, seeing your very great love for each other, seeing that these actions are actions of love, one toward the other, and not just the expression of physical passion, may find that it is right. But there is a limit in engagements.

PENITENT: Is the limit that one mustn't perform the complete act? But can we do all the other things that are close to it, but aren't the complete marriage act?

PRIEST: Yes, I'm telling you that. Because the Church hasn't said anything very exact. You'll find many priests who are stricter than I am in this field. But I believe the rule should be this, first of all because it's not that you are far from God during this engagement of yours—you, after all, are good to your fiancé, you're conscientious, you ought to feel that there's a certain limit, because if you did things properly, not only would you end up by doing the full act, but—

PENITENT: We might have children.

PRIEST: Exactly. You could have children. There are two things, aren't there? There is this total joy, this living together which I would say, at least according to the profounder sense of things, cannot be repeated—because it's not that a girl tries first with one and then leaves him and repeats it with another—because there's an intimacy which ... grows almost within the flesh.

PENITENT: Yes, because if I were to realize, now, that we

didn't get along, it would be much better to end it, naturally, and not commit—

PRIEST: Just a minute. You talk about ending it. In that case you realize the value of this law, don't you? A girl who has had full intimacy with her fiancé goes away diminished.

PENITENT: If she realizes that she's marrying the wrong man, it's better to leave him, isn't it?

PRIEST: I agree. But, you see, I'd say to a young man who asked me what you are asking, "Look, you want to preserve a certain amount of freedom so you can send this girl away if you don't get along together?" He'd say, "Yes." And I would add, "Wouldn't you want to send her away the way she was when you met her? Then you can't use her as if you were flesh of each other's flesh because you are not yet completely united." After all, there is a limit of respect, at least at the extreme, that must impose itself upon every conscience.

PENITENT: Yes, but a priest I confessed to some time ago said that it was a sin even to kiss. Well, explain that to me. I really don't understand, it seems so silly.

PRIEST: Well, that idea means that all pleasure, let's say sensual pleasure—not that sensual pleasures are sinful, because they, too, come from God—has to be within marriage. So, a kiss, given on the mouth, and prolonged, seeking an effect on the senses, was considered bad.

PENITENT: But that was in the past!

PRIEST: Many still think that way. I believe that two engaged people like you who love each other, who take care of each other, moving forward toward marriage . . . At the beginning, reserve is very important, and then, as one goes on, it gets more difficult, I'd say it's almost normal that certain acts take place at a certain point. Try to do the best you can, to give your fiancé peace from this point of view. When you see that there's a certain physical tension, see if you can keep it within bounds. And if you really can't, it will mean that you have allowed yourself to be carried away, as it were, but it's not a good thing because it goes beyond the bounds of engagement. Do you understand what I've said?

PENITENT: Yes, I understand.

PRIEST: It seems that there isn't any more to say. I try to put myself in your place. As you said, two people who truly love each other as you two do . . . naturally, I understand that there comes a time—

PENITENT: We think it's a natural thing and not something that can lead to evil. Do you see?

PRIEST: I'd **say**, rather, that one ought to think about the harm that you may do yourselves because of the nature of engagement, which is a state of transition, isn't it? Let's say that you live with your fiancé . . . I know a girl who is actually living with her fiancé and he's kept her waiting for ten years. Now, I have urged her to be firm and so on. But the difficulty lies in the girl herself. When they're together she can't resist because, in short, physical love is a very strong thing. Now I would say that a girl ought not to become such a victim of physical love, of this man who has introduced her to love. Now, she herself says, "Yes, I never should have gone beyond a certain limit. I would have felt much freer toward him, maybe I would have left him long ago, and by now I might have had my own family, my own children. I went too far."

PENITENT: But isn't it opportunistic to reason like that?

PRIEST: Well, more than opportunistic.

PENITENT: It's like saying, "I'll act pure, so as to make him marry me."

PRIEST: No, no, it wasn't that. She didn't say she should have acted pure so as to get married. She said that it was harder, afterward, to leave him because the union with this man had become part of her being.

PENITENT: Well, then, how am I to act in the future? I don't intend to change, in the sense that . . . What do you advise me to do?

PRIEST: When do you intend to marry?

PENITENT: Oh, I don't know, in a few years' time.

PRIEST: Well, I must say . . . I don't know . . . above all, don't abandon the sacraments.

PENITENT: Can I take Communion even though I'm in this situation?

PRIEST: You should promise, within yourself, to Our Lord, that you will not let yourself go fully, that you won't lose sight of the limits in the expression of your love, that you will try to remain—

PENITENT: Just a minute, I'd like to understand what you mean by limits. The full act?

PRIEST: Yes. But the complete act is also prepared by acts of intimacy very close to the complete act, isn't it? I think that being close to one another, with a certain normal physical intimacy, doesn't mean anything bad. But to go further is to go against the laws of prudence and moral health. I think that you can promise this to Our Lord.

PENITENT: Even if I know that I am going to fall again?

PRIEST: Well, yes. A person can think that they may succeed, or may not. But to foresee that you may fall doesn't signify that you don't mean well.

PENITENT: It's the good intention that counts.

PRIEST: Yes, that's it. I'd say the Lord loves you both and is glad about your love. The Lord wants a certain amount of reserve, because of a lot of reasons, which He made Himself.

PENITENT: All right.

PRIEST: We have had a nice talk.

PENITENT: Yes, Father, I thank you.

PRIEST: There's nothing to thank me for. Have you heard mass?

PENITENT: Yes.

PRIEST: Will you take Communion?

PENITENT: I will, tomorrow morning.

PRIEST: Very well, I'll give you absolution. I have confidence, great confidence in this love of yours.

CHURCH OF SAN GIUSEPPE, MILAN

PRIEST: How long is it since you confessed?

PENITENT: A few months, I don't remember.

PRIEST: Did you confess regularly before?

PENITENT: Yes, fairly.

PRIEST: Why have you waited so long? Do you have any crisis of a spiritual nature? Is there something wrong?

PENITENT: Yes, I'm engaged and I've had intimate relations with my girl friend, and since I know that the Church doesn't allow this, I haven't been to confession.

PRIEST: And why have you come now to confess?

PENITENT: I came to get an opinion, rather than to confess, to find out if my fears were justified.

PRIEST: Well, my son, the problem is not as insoluble as you think, did you know that? The problem is much simpler. You can't have intimate relations with your fiancée before you're married, because that is God's law. The law God gave to men does not permit it, you see. But man is a weak creature, and he can easily make mistakes. It's enough that a person should admit his mistake and promise not to do it any more, do you see? The Lord admits the error and in His immense goodness He forgives it.

PENITENT: Put like that, it seems easy. But the problem is a different one. I am not at all convinced that I'm making a mistake. My fiancée and I have these relations, we desire them, and we feel that they're necessary in order to test the exact degree of our sexual harmony.

PRIEST: But, my son, don't you think about the consequences? And what if you bring a child into the world in these, shall we say, abnormal conditions?

PENITENT: We've been careful. We have relations only in the periods when my fiancée is infertile.

PRIEST: But, I mean, do you do the full act?

PENITENT: Almost always, yes, but sometimes not.

PRIEST: That is, you leave it inside her?

PENITENT: Yes, why?

PRIEST: But, my son, the Lord cannot approve these things before you have been consecrated by marriage.

PENITENT: That's just what I wanted to know. By acting in this way must I consider myself outside the Church?

PRIEST: [*Long pause*] I myself wouldn't be so ... I mean, I wouldn't pose the problem in such drastic terms. You, my son, must try to think about things. You must hold yourself in, because grace is a gift from God that we cannot refuse in such a lighthearted way. If you try hard—

PENITENT: I haven't made myself clear, Father. I might, if I tried hard, as you say, manage not to have intimate relations. But that's not what I want. I don't think that makes sense. During our engagement, my girl friend and I have to find out whether there's a chance of understanding as a character, sensitivity, but also sensuality.

PRIEST: But all that's needed for that is a premarital examination and the problem is solved, wisely and—

PENITENT: No, no, Father. It's obvious that you know nothing at all about these problems. My girl friend and I are two completely normal people, perfectly all right sexually. That's not the problem as you seem to think. I'll explain it to you more clearly. My fiancée and I are sexually normal, like most people. And we get along well as regards to character. With other girls, equally normal, with whom I tried before, our characters clashed. The same thing happens from the sexual point of view. Two completely normal people can achieve perfect sexual harmony. Two people, equally normal, can be a disaster, sexually. The premarital examination can't do anything about that. Only direct experience counts.

PRIEST: Yes, my son. But now that you've had this experience, that's sufficient, isn't it?

PENITENT: The longer the experience goes on, the more valid

it is. Anyway, as I said, I don't see anything wrong in it.

PRIEST: Well, then, you're reducing the engagement period to a sort of anticipated marriage. Does that seem right to you?

PENITENT: But that isn't exactly so. Marriage forms a family, engagement doesn't. Marriage gives the pleasure of living together. Aren't those sufficient differences, in your opinion?

PRIEST: Listen, my son, I could give you absolution but you will have to put your conscience in order directly with God.

PENITENT: But excuse me, Father, I'm studying medicine, and I can't afford to marry until I'm over thirty. Do you really think that a man can arrive at that age a virgin? Do you really believe that?

PRIEST: Of course not. But a few mistakes are permitted. They can be forgiven.

PENITENT: But it's hypocritical to call a need a mistake. And the rule, in our case, would be continence, a condition that even you, Father, admit is impossible to maintain.

PRIEST: I agree. [*Long pause*] But if a person really can't do without, there are other remedies.

PENITENT: What other remedies? Masturbation?

PRIEST: I don't know. If a person really can't do without, there are streetwalkers, don't you see?

PENITENT: But you, Father, advise this?

PRIEST: My son, I don't advise anything, I was just saying . . . However, if you feel that it's all right and honest to do what you're doing, go on doing it. After all, I understand you. It's less harmful for a man than it is for a woman. But if your fiancée agrees, and if she doesn't see anything wrong in it, all right, I'll give you absolution just the same. Are you satisfied?

PENITENT: I thank you, Father.

PRIEST: As penance say five Hail Marys. Act of Contrition.

## CONCLUSION:
## PRIESTS OUT OF TOUCH WITH LIFE

It isn't necessary to quote psychologists to emphasize the estrangement the priest feels when he is faced with the problems of a believer today. A few voices within the Church itself have expressed the problem clearly.

Father Carl Morandin, a Benedictine counselor to the Theological Association of Moralists, says: "Love is dynamic relationship that grows and perfects itself. Is the sacrament that codifies it to be fixed at one moment of formal ritual or rather when the two people reach their perfection of love? This is something that can happen not only *after* the marriage ceremony but also *before.*

"The exclusion of full intercourse between engaged people was understandable when it was also held that sex was solely for procreation. But it is understandable no longer," Father Morandin explains, "if we assign other dimensions to the sexual aspect of a relationship."

# IV

## OLDER WOMEN ALONE

MILLIONS OF older women live without any continual sexual relationship. The unmarried, the widows, and the separated wives are a "loveless army" that have to fall back on either love affairs with themselves or lives of promiscuity.

We asked ninety-six priests what the Church attitude was toward an older woman alone. Unanimously, the priests insisted that the only answer was a life of absolute chastity. Of these, thirty-six priests seemed to understand the unhappiness of the penitent, but even they could not advise that she follow her own conscience and ask for forgiveness directly from God.

### ABSOLUTE CHASTITY

*Out of the sixty conversations in which the priests told the women questioners "absolute chastity and that's all," we report the full text of those which seem to us to be the most representative.*

CHURCH OF SAN GIOVANNI, PALERMO

PRIEST: Jesus Christ be praised.

PENITENT: May He always be praised.

PRIEST: Tell me about the sins you've committed since your last confession.

PENITENT: I really want to ask advice, rather than make a confession.

PRIEST: Go ahead.

PENITENT: I find myself in an unhappy situation that's kept me from the Church for some time. You see, I am almost forty, and not married. Recently I met a man. We love each other and we've started an affair although we can't marry because he's been separated for ten years. I was very unhappy for a long time beforehand, because I needed affection and had physiological needs that I couldn't repress. Now, I feel well, I'm happy. There's only one snag . . . I'm afraid of being outside the Church.

PRIEST: You are not, but you are in a state of sin. God's law does not envisage relations of a conjugal nature outside marriage without God's blessing.

PENITENT: Yes, but I have never had a chance to get married, unfortunately. It's not that I didn't want to, I wasn't able to, that's all.

PRIEST: But, listen, did you reach the age of forty . . . without—

PENITENT: Without what? What do you know, Father, about what it's cost me to arrive at this age without a sound emotional and sexual relationship?

PRIEST: Did you seek pleasure by yourself?

PENITENT: Well . . . yes.

PRIEST: How?

PENITENT: The way people do in such cases.

PRIEST: I mean with caresses in your most delicate parts, exciting caresses, accompanied by unhealthy thoughts?

PENITENT: Oh, I don't know. Maybe. Why do you want to know about that, Father?

PRIEST: Because it gives me a chance to ascertain the nature and character of your sensuality. You see, my dear, if you merely engaged in caressing and exciting with your hands, you committed an acceptable sin. That is, it comes almost spontaneously, and God can understand it. But if you have done other things, that's another matter.

PENITENT: I don't understand you, Father.

PRIEST: I mean that if you have sought pleasure, orgasm, with other instruments, artificial instruments pushed into the vagina, then your sin is much more serious, do you understand? And also, there is the danger of serious physical consequences. That's what I mean. It is no longer natural, that's all.

PENITENT: No, Father, nothing of that kind. I never even thought of it. But do such things happen?

PRIEST: Well, you know, in the confessional we hear about all human frailties, and there are these things as well!

PENITENT: Well, anyway, Father, let's get back to my case. Now I've found this relationship that completes me. It makes me feel alive and I don't want to give it up.

PRIEST: But you can never again be in the grace of God if you accept a situation as false as this one will always be!

PENITENT: So, then, you think the situation I was in before was better, with neurosis, loneliness, obtaining satisfaction from time to time by myself?

PRIEST: No, that's not the right situation either. But, if nothing else, in that way you do not involve another person in sin.

PENITENT: But why "involve in sin"? That's what I don't understand. I love him and he loves me. What's more, he's begun proceedings for a divorce. I can't understand why I should give up a bit of serenity. For whom? For what?

PRIEST: For God.

PENITENT: Thank you, Father, all right.

PRIEST: What are you doing? You're leaving like that?

PENITENT: Yes, because you've confirmed what I feared. You see, Father, I'm losing my faith in God, little by little, just because you give me an image of God that I no longer receive. I refuse to believe that a God can condemn me to a life of hell, just because it's a sin to have relations with a married man even though he has been separated from his wife for ten years. If I were destroying a family, I might be able to understand the condemnation. But the way it is, no, Father. I'm not. We're not hurting anyone, don't you see?

PRIEST: My dear, one can't make laws case by case. God's law is universal and goes for everyone. I agree, there may be cases in which it may seem unjust, but no law is always and absolutely just.

PENITENT: That's so. But priests ought to have the power of discretion in applying it.

PRIEST: They do, but up to a certain point. In fact, I don't feel like condemning you, and maybe not even God condemns you. But I can't give you absolution, you know. I tell you that you are not outside the Church, and that the Church awaits you . . . is waiting for something in your life to change, I mean.

PENITENT: All right, Father. I thank you.

PRIEST: Don't be discouraged, continue to pray to God and to behave as your conscience suggests. You'll see that you won't regret it.

CHURCH OF SANTO STEFANO, SAN REMO

PRIEST: May Jesus Christ be praised.
PENITENT: May He always be praised.
PRIEST: How long is it since you confessed?
PENITENT: I don't know, a long time.
PRIEST: Months?
PENITENT: Yes.

PRIEST: Did you do your Easter duties?

PENITENT: No.

PRIEST: How's that? Why?

PENITENT: I find myself in a special situation, Father. I'm no longer very young, I'm thirty-nine, and I've met a man who's separated from his wife. So, I've decided to live with him. I'm a Catholic, I'm a believer, but there comes a time . . . I see the years going by. I'd like to ask your advice. I don't know whether you can understand me.

PRIEST: By God's grace I shall try to understand you. So, you are separated from this man?

PENITENT: No, no, you haven't understood. I'm unmarried, he's the one who's separated from his wife.

PRIEST: Well, then, all you can do is break it off.

PENITENT: No, I don't want to break it off, I want to go on. I mean, we've begun now and I don't want to lose these last years of my life . . . of my young life, let's say.

PRIEST: But don't you realize that you'll lose your serenity, your tranquillity? And then you must take into account the man's wife.

PENITENT: But they've been separated for years now. It has nothing to do with me at all.

PRIEST: Yes it does. Because if you marry him, there'll be no further chances of his reuniting with his wife.

PENITENT: But he's completely estranged from her for many years. Anyway, she's living with another man. But that's not the problem. The problem is, well, I want that little bit of happiness that love can give me. Because I haven't made any vow of chastity.

PRIEST: I understand you. You're a woman who hasn't become a nun and who can't find a husband. So what do you want to do about it? Find just any man?

PENITENT: No, I found the man I love and I don't see why it can't be . . . I don't think that Our Lord, so good and merciful, can condemn me.

PRIEST: Yes, He does condemn you. Definitely. Because Jesus in the gospel condemns even thoughts of these things. Yes, because even the thought, the desire, to be with that man is already adultery and therefore a very grave sin. It's a serious offense against that woman who is his wife.

PENITENT: But that woman doesn't exist, she had ceased to exist even before we met. We're happy together.

PRIEST: No, don't say that. That way of speaking is not human, let alone Christian. You're a cruel woman, madam. Think of the wife.

PENITENT: But why should I think of her? She no longer exists, she has another family now. What does she have to do with it?

PRIEST: A good deal.

PENITENT: But I don't understand why you insist on this. That woman no longer exists, she lives in another town, she's made a new life for herself. And a long time before I even knew about her.

PRIEST: That doesn't matter. That woman belongs to this man, and this man belongs to that woman.

PENITENT: But only in law, because in reality they don't belong to each other at all. Anyway, the problem concerns me and not that woman. I don't care anything about her. What I want to say is, I haven't done anything wrong. I've found this man who's been alone for years, I love him and he loves me and I don't see why, in these last years while I'm fairly young, I shouldn't—

PRIEST: Enjoy the satisfaction of a relationship, right?

PENITENT: Exactly! And also because, after a certain period of psychological crisis, due to loneliness, even my doctor advised me to have a normal sentimental and sexual relationship.

PRIEST: Yes.

PENITENT: Does it seem right to you that I should fall back into an even worse crisis, after having known what it is to be happy, just . . . just because of what?

PRIEST: Look. You are unhappy now, but if you go with that man, you won't just be unhappy within yourself, but also in the eyes of others.

PENITENT: I don't believe that. Because we're not hurting anyone. We love each other. Indeed, we're happy, we're content. I can't see what harm we're doing.

PRIEST: You're harming him and you're harming yourself. You're harming him because you're leading him along a mistaken path and if he dies he will go to hell. You're harming yourself because practically speaking you're selling your body to a man who will exploit all that there is that's young and will leave you by the roadside. Just as he left his wife, he will leave you.

PENITENT: But that doesn't have to happen. But anyway, I will have lived happily for a few years, I'll have had my share of living.

PRIEST: Our Lord says in His holy laws that the woman who has not found marriage must offer Him the sacrifice of her chastity.

PENITENT: But why should He ask that of me? It's not fair.

PRIEST: Yes, He wants this from you because life has its commitments—human life, but above all Christian life. It has commitments of honor and honesty, commitments of peace, commitments with God. We have to account to God for all that we feel and experience.

PENITENT: To be in peace with God, then, one has to be unhappy.

PRIEST: Yes, certainly you must be unhappy, leave him. Definitely. Why do you want to cause remorse? No, look. To abandon yourself to a blind, sensual love would be the end. If you leave him, though, you'll be doing good. If you really love him, you must tell him, "Stay where you should be, because you are married."

PENITENT: But he's asking for a divorce. The marriage then will be finished.

PRIEST: And you, poor woman, want to enjoy these sensual pleasures?

PENITENT: It's not just a question of sensual pleasures. It's a lot of things. To live with a man doesn't just mean going to bed, even though that's important, because physiological needs do exist. God put them in our bodies, didn't He?

PRIEST: Look, you must think about the consequences of this step. Of course it may solve certain problems. But it might create others much more serious, such as the loss of your interior peace, the disagreements that may arise with this man. Then the affection and esteem of his relatives may be at stake. Is it really worthwhile to risk all that?

PENITENT: Father, I don't know whether you are young or old, and I suppose that you have some experience, but I don't feel like a black sheep. Or am I one?

PRIEST: Oh, no. There are many cases. You're not the first, poor woman, who has allowed herself to be embroiled by this desire to be married at all costs. But one must not be obsessed with this idea.

PENITENT: But what if a person can't get married?

PRIEST: They must seek other interests. Life is made up of so many other things. You must try to occupy your time with activities.

PENITENT: Oh, but I do all kinds of things. I work, I've got many interests, but it's not enough, Father. Do you understand? It's not enough for me.

PRIEST: But there are other satisfactions. You can come here to me, we can do some good, spiritually too. We can devote ourselves to the care of some child, we can do some welfare work, we can try to give our love—

PENITENT: But one can't always be doing this. Anyway, why did God give us bodies? To mortify them?

PRIEST: And why not? Of course, for that also. When one doesn't find legitimate solutions.

PENITENT: But it's not fair, and since God is justice, I don't believe that's what He wants.

PRIEST: Well, then, all those people who aren't married ought to reason—to rebel the same way you do.

PENITENT: Don't you think that inside they do rebel? All the nervous disorders that exist, what causes them? What do you think?

PRIEST: There are more internal rebellions in those that marry than in those that don't.

PENITENT: It seems to me, Father, that you don't know about human beings.

PRIEST: One must consider the thing with intelligence—

PENITENT: But in this case intelligence only counts to a certain point.

PRIEST: —and understand that it's necessary to respect other people's freedom. You would be limiting the freedom of that man already married, don't you see?

PENITENT: But I don't impose anything on him. We decide things together. And I know that I'd make him happy. Because he's not happy now. He suffers from loneliness, as I do. Do you know what I mean?

PRIEST: Yes, I understand. But vice does harm to the body.

PENITENT: But why "vice"?

PRIEST: It brings nothing good.

PENITENT: Why do you say that? I don't understand you at all, you know. You presuppose bad faith in both of us, but we really love each other and—

PRIEST: But he's separated from his wife.

PENITENT: There are lots of reasons for that. So many marriages break up, and neither one nor both of the partners is to blame.

PRIEST: I say that there are other satisfactions besides that of getting married. If that were the only one, then all those who married would be happy. Instead, they talk of divorce. In Italy seventy per cent would like to divorce, they want to go with another woman, and then to leave *her,* and so on. Where would we end up? You see, it's not that marriages bring happiness.

PENITENT: I don't claim that marriage guarantees happiness.

PRIEST: Matrimony is an experience that gives us, always, only a part of what we expected. I don't see why anyone should desire it in such a paroxysmal way.

PENITENT: But, Father, I have the right to the affection of a man, and to give him my affection. If he's not my husband, never mind, just as long as our relationship is based on honesty and we don't harm anyone.

PRIEST: But God doesn't want this.

PENITENT: I don't believe that He doesn't want ... I mean, if He is infinite goodness, infinite justice, if he knows everything—

PRIEST: But infinite justice means God's justice, according to what Our Lord has taught us and asked us to do. You must not play about with God's justice, young lady. There are many people who are not married, and yet they're happy just the same. They find the way to give love and help to others.

PENITENT: But I've tried, and I haven't found that happiness.

PRIEST: And yet, experience teaches us this ... We, who have been so many, may well say so.

PENITENT: Listen, Father, I don't feel I can promise you that I'll leave this man, just because of the convictions that I've expressed to you. I'd like to be a good Catholic just the same. But I don't feel that I have to renounce life and love and mortify my senses and my instincts to be one. I really don't feel I can promise you that.

PRIEST: You must think it over carefully, because in doing what you're doing, you're refusing the grace of God. You prove that you have no respect for yourself or your family. What will your parents think about it? You mother? Your mother could die of a broken heart. There are grave and painful consequences.

PENITENT: My parents are dead, and my relatives care so little about me that they certainly won't feel any moral uneasiness if I go live with a married man. There's no problem. The question is something else. Can I still be a good Catholic and go to church, the way things are?

PRIEST: You can still go to church, but you won't be a good Catholic, that's all. Anyway, think it over, consider what you are about to do, pray to God for enlightenment, and then come back so we can discuss it again.

PENITENT: All right, Father, Thank you.

## CHURCH OF SANTA MARIA DELLE GRAZIE, NAPLES

PRIEST: How long is it since you confessed, my child?

PENITENT: I don't remember exactly, about two or three months.

PRIEST: What sins have you committed?

PENITENT: I've missed mass on Sundays.

PRIEST: Often?

PENITENT: No, no.

PRIEST: And then?

PENITENT: Maybe I haven't always been courteous and understanding toward others. I've had some nervous outbursts.

PRIEST: It's necessary to control oneself, my child. Never lose one's temper because, in such cases one draws near to the beasts, which do not reason and don't have the gift of intelligence. Are they frequent, child, these nervous outbursts?

PENITENT: Well, yes.

PRIEST: Do you not feel at peace within yourself, my child? What is wrong?

PENITENT: I don't know . . . really . . .

PRIEST: Are you married?

PENITENT: No.

PRIEST: How old are you?

PENITENT: Forty.

PRIEST: Is there some friendship, child, of a . . . let's say . . . intimate nature? With some man?

PENITENT: I did have, but not any longer.

PRIEST: And is this what makes you nervous?

PENITENT: That as well, certainly.

PRIEST: Are you a sensual woman, my child? Do you have repressed desires?

PENITENT: But . . .

PRIEST: You may speak quite frankly. I hear so much in this place! Before you, this morning, there was a lady of fifty who was upset on account of an erotic relationship with a sixteen-year-old boy, the son of one of her best friends. She told me everything. We discussed it, my child, both of us blushing, but in the end she went away feeling calmer, more serene, more . . . determined to end it. [*Long pause*] Well, my child, do you have repressed desires that torment you?

PENITENT: Well, yes. It's natural at my age, isn't it?

PRIEST: And what do you do about them?

PENITENT: I try to control myself . . . and then, when I can't any longer, then . . .

PRIEST: Then? Come on, courage.

PENITENT: Well, I do it by myself.

PRIEST: I understand, because I'm a sinner too, did you know that? I feel certain desires, did you know that? It's in our nature, you see. But we must try to control them, to reduce them through reasoning and use of will power, as well as through prayer and God's help. But what is it exactly you do, my child?

PENITENT: I don't know, what can I say to you?

PRIEST: Everything. When is it that you feel "restless" in a particular way? In the evening, in bed? In the spring? After reading indecent books or having seen immoral films?

PENITENT: Well, yes, that's the way it is.

PRIEST: You caress yourself with your hands, or do you use . . . other gadgets?

PENITENT: What does it matter?

PRIEST: With the hands is a more natural thing, my child. If you use instruments that one sees advertised nowadays one

arrives at true sadism, which is a horror to God. Do you understand my child?

PENITENT: I don't use those things.

PRIEST: Have you ever done it with a girl friend? I mean, have
you had homosexual relations?

PENITENT: Only once. I gave in, but I've never done it again.

PRIEST: You did right to stop because it's disastrous, my child,
when one lowers oneself to such baseness. And with animals, my
child, do you do filthy things with animals?

PENITENT: Oh, no, Father!

PRIEST: And you succeed, by yourself, in satisfying your
desires fully. Do you feel satisfied afterward?

PENITENT: Sometimes yes and sometimes no. You see,
Father, I'm a sensual woman, as you say, but I'm healthy too.
It's not sex that I desire, but also affection. Alone, I can satisfy
the first, at least partly. But a man, a complete relationship.
affectionate and sexual at the same time. But I can't find any
men who are free, who suit me. So I must content myself with
having a relationship with a man who's either separated or
divorced. That's better, isn't it, than doing things by oneself?

PRIEST: No, my child, you must not do this. If you do, you
leave the bosom of the Church.

PENITENT: Why?

PRIEST: Because God does not wish this. This is only possible,
my child, within marriage. You see, I, too, have sexual problems, and if God permitted it I would marry as Protestant
clergymen do. But God does not permit it, and so I resign myself, with His aid, and it's understood.

PENITENT: And how do you deal with your sexual problems?

PRIEST: Alas, human nature is weak, but we must gain
strength from prayer and—

PENITENT: Do you succeed?

PRIEST: Well, almost always. However, in these cases, it's best
to manage by oneself, do you understand, my child? It's better

that way because then you don't involve others and cause others to sin, you see.

PENITENT: But isn't it more unnatural?

PRIEST: Unnatural is unnatural, child, but between the two evils . . . When you caress yourself, what do you think about, eh?

PENITENT: I don't know. I feel pleasure.

PRIEST: Well, I'll tell you, my dear child, you think . . . your fingers, in those moments are . . . represent the male penis, which is moving between your thighs. You feel pleasure because of this, my child. So, these acts—that God does not approve, of course—are less unnatural than you think. You are committing a sin, my child, but a lesser sin than having relations with a man who is not your husband. Do you understand?

PENITENT: No, I don't understand that. I could understand it if it were a matter of purely physical contact, two people who just meet once to satisfy their sexual instincts. But if there's real love, a mutual exchange of love, which can't end in marriage for reasons beyond one's control, well, then, I don't think it's a sin.

PRIEST: It is a sin, my child, it is a sin. And a grave one too. I, as a priest, can close an eye to masturbation by a woman of your age, certainly tormented by sexual abstinence. It still is a sin, my child. I could not absolve you if you had an illicit relationship with a man. You, child, tell me that this is not fair, but it is not for us, miserable sinners, to decide what is just and what is not. Do you see?

PENITENT: I see, Father, and I thank you for this explanation. So, must I go on as I have been doing?

PRIEST: Pray, pray often, ask God for the strength to resist even this solitary love. If you don't succeed, confess your sin, come to me, my dear child, and we will speak about it again with the same serenity with which we have spoken today. It will do you good, child. In the end your ideas will become clearer, you'll see. Trust in me.

PENITENT: Will you give me absolution?

PRIEST: Not this time, no, because you still have to be convinced of what I have told you, child. For today I give you only the blessing of Our Lord. But if you return, you'll see, I'll come to giving you absolution. You'll see.

PENITENT: Thank you, Father.

*The following are the most interesting extracts from other conversations in which the priest expressed himself in equally uncompromising terms.*

## CHURCH OF SANTA MARIA SOPRA MINERVA, ROME

PENITENT: Father, It's been about a month since I last confessed. I'm thirty-nine and unmarried. My problem seems to be rather a big one. I never had any relations with men. I don't know whether it's more sinful to do that or to go with him, you see. I don't know.

PRIEST: It's rather a serious matter. It will take some time. You must understand. Obviously, you don't mind my asking, do you?

PENITENT: What is it I'm supposed to understand?

PRIEST: Eh, this thing . . . this man, that you know. How do you know him? With what aim, with what purpose?

PENITENT: He's a person who lives near me, who moves in the same circles I do.

PRIEST: Is he married?

PENITENT: No, he's separated.

PRIEST: Well, he's still married then. It's a question of discovering whether you, at your age, can find a person who is free to marry.

PENITENT: But I've never found anyone up till now! I want to know, in fact, whether it's a bigger sin—

PRIEST: It's not a question of a bigger or a lesser sin. It's a question of morality, and morality speaks plainly.

PENITENT: In other words, I'm not to go with this man, but I can seek satisfaction on my own?

PRIEST: No, no, you mustn't do that either.

PENITENT: All right, but I'm unhappy. Even the doctor advised me to seek a relationship.

PRIEST: The doctor acted wrongly in this because, permit me to say so, a doctor is supposed to know about morality as well as about medicine.

PENITENT: Yes, all right, but if, on the other hand, my organism needs—

PRIEST: No-o-o!

PENITENT: —certain impulses?

PRIEST: If everyone reasoned like that where would Christian virtue be?

PENITENT: All right, but I've tried to control myself for years and now I'm half neurotic.

PRIEST: And what is it that causes this neurosis?

PRIEST: It's caused by this repression of the impulses from my organism, by the strain that comes from continual self-control.

PRIEST: That's not true, young lady. If you reason—

PENITENT: But the Church . . . I mean, this thing isn't unique. There are so many women in the same situation as I am, with the same problems, aren't there?

PRIEST: These problems that you have can be those also of nuns, who are not married.

PENITENT: All right, but they have an ideal for which they've taken a vow of chastity. I haven't made such a vow.

PRIEST: But if you don't find your ideal, naturally you end up with a neurosis. So it's an aim you have to achieve. One cannot remain inert in the face of this reasoning: I won't do this because I want to do this other thing, right?

PENITENT: I know, but if I don't find a husband?

PRIEST: Oh, yes, you will find one.

PENITENT: But if I haven't found one so far! If I were twenty, all right.

PRIEST: Listen. Can we talk about this a little later?

PENITENT: Anyway, what I wanted to know was if it happens, from time to time, that I—

PRIEST: I can hear that there are a lot of people waiting to confess. We can discuss it, if you wait until later, when I've finished with the people who are waiting—

## CHURCH DELLA PACE, BRESCIA

PENITENT: Yes, Father. But you see, at my age, I have no chance whatsoever of getting married. But I need a relationship that's physiologically and sentimentally sound, and this man could give me that, because we love each other.

PRIEST: But he's married.

PENITENT: Yes, but he's been separated for seven years now, and his wife lives abroad.

PRIEST: That doesn't alter anything, the bond remains.

PENITENT: But what's a lonely woman like me to do, then? Chastity all her life? Father, do you really believe that such a thing is possible, the way things are today?

PRIEST: Excuse me, but what have you done until now? How did you arrive at the age you are now?

PENITENT: Mortifying myself with—how shall I say it?—with personal satisfaction.

PRIEST: And did you get pleasure out of it?

PENITENT: It's just an outlet. But don't you understand that I'm a woman like all others, it's just that I haven't had the luck to find a man to marry. The men of my generation fought in the war, and a lot died, do you understand?

PRIEST: If you have faith, if you believe in God's law, you must accept the sacrifice of chastity with serenity, peacefully. Maybe you can devote yourself to other interests, committing yourself to—

PENITENT: I do have faith, otherwise I wouldn't be here. But there comes a time when it's difficult to believe in something that forces you to be unhappy without giving you a logical reason for it. Do you see?

PRIEST: Yes, I do.

PENITENT: Anyway, Father, which is the bigger sin, the seeking of a stable relationship, even one not blessed by the Church, or to resign myself to these personal outlets?

PRIEST: Well, it's a sin in both cases. You can't have a bigger or a smaller sin. Certainly a relationship with a man is more natural, but it is more blameworthy since it involves another person. One can't advise "to do this, or do that." I can tell you to pray to Our Lord and ask Him for the strength to control yourself, to find a balance without breaking His law, that's all. Yes, that's all I can tell you; the rest is up to your conscience and, yes, your courage, too.

## CHASTITY, YES, BUT...

*In thirty-six of the recorded conversations, the priest, while emphasizing the Church's stand of demanding absolute chastity outside of marriage, showed himself prepared to accept a more broad-minded and constructive solution.*

CHURCH OF SAN LORENZO, AGRIGENTO

PRIEST: How long is it since you confessed?

PENITENT: About a couple of months. Father, I find myself in a special situation. I'm thirty-eight now and I've never been engaged or married, nothing. Now I've met a man who's separated from his wife. I've decided to go live with him, but since I'm a Catholic, I'd like to have your advice.

PRIEST: But he can't marry you since he's already married, right?

PENITENT: He's married and separated from his wife.

PRIEST: Now tell me, does he have children?

PENITENT: Yes, but they're grown up.

PRIEST: I see. This is counsel that's very hard to give. A woman who's Catholic cannot live with a man without a regular marriage.

PENITENT: But I've reached an age when I don't expect to get married any more, and besides, I haven't made a vow of chastity.

PRIEST: That's true, but what can one do? At the most you can ask him to promise that he'll put things right, should the other party die, let's say.

PENITENT: All right, but what if she doesn't die? I mean, can we have a normal relationship, a complete one, in the meantime?

PRIEST: As if you were husband and wife?

PENITENT: Yes, surely.

PRIEST: Naturally, not just from time to time, because it must be stable or nothing. But in any case, it would be necessary to . . . Is he legally separated?

PENITENT: Yes.

PRIEST: He's legally separated. I see. These situations are really rather unpleasant, you know. Even the confessor doesn't know what advice to give. You should not live with anyone. But as you quite rightly say, you have not made any vow of chastity, and you are perfectly right. I can't tell you not to live with him, you see, because it's something truly human. But you might wait a bit. Who knows, you might find someone who's not married, I don't know, one who can regularize—

PENITENT: But we're in love now. And anyway, at my age, I really don't think I'm likely to find anyone!

PRIEST: How old are you?

PENITENT: Thirty-eight.

PRIEST: Well, there are people even older than that who have married.

PENITENT: All right, but I don't want to get married just for the sake of getting married.

PRIEST: What do you want, young lady? Do as you think best, all right? The Lord is merciful, and He sees and reads people's hearts. You're in love, aren't you? Do as you think best, then. The important thing is that you should not give up your prayers and that you should approach the sacraments just the same.

PENITENT: But can I approach the sacraments when I'm having relations with this man? That's what I want to know.

PRIEST: Oh, well, the sacraments. You keep on confessing, and you'll find some broad-minded confessor. Because these are situations that—

PENITENT: But shall I find a priest who will give me absolution?

PRIEST: Who knows? This is not a good position to be in. Anyway, you're already living with this man?

PENITENT: No, not yet, but I've decided to do it.

PRIEST: I see.

PENITENT: And, then, there's always the possibility of divorce.

PRIEST: Young lady, I don't think the Church will ever consider it. To open up a loophole of that kind would mean the opening of many others. And I think that divorce—

PENITENT: But from the civic point of view it's something—

PRIEST: It's a thorn in the relations between Church and state.

PENITENT: But why? For what reason?

PRIEST: Because it's in contrast with the Concordat. Anyway, I'm of the opinion that the matrimonial cases should be dealt with by the Church with a certain speed so as to arrive at a complete loosening of the bond of the Church's part.

PENITENT: Yes, but there are only those three or four kinds of cases in which the Church dissolves marriage. The chances for annulment ought to be broadened, then.

PRIEST: Yes, broadened. In fact, as I was saying, they ought to be broadened and speeded up, because at present they take too long. Infidelity, for instance, should be accepted as a cause for dissolving marriage.

PENITENT: And sexual incompatibility, too.

PRIEST: Sexual incompatibility, and incompatibility of character as well.

PENITENT: Do you think that there's a trend of thought within the Church in that direction?

PRIEST: Yes, there is, there is. Quite a lot.

PENITENT: I haven't read anything about it.

PRIEST: Oh, lots of things don't get published. There's something brewing, though. Let's hope it comes through. Certainly there are some situations that are really terrible, so that even the confessor doesn't know what to say. What can I tell you? Do as you think best, because the Lord is merciful. He sees people's intentions. I can't say more than that.

PENITENT: I see. Well, anyway, thank you.

PRIEST: You're welcome. Have you done your religious duties?

PENITENT: To tell the truth, no.

PRIEST: But have you already had sexual relations with this man?

PENITENT: Yes.

PRIEST: Well, ask the Lord's forgiveness with all your heart. Try to repent. What can I say to you?

PENITENT: But, Father, it's not a question of repentance. I find that these things are natural, therefore I don't feel that I'm committing a sin.

PRIEST: Yes, I know they are natural things, seeing that you're already living as man and wife. They are natural things, yes.

PENITENT: Well, I mean, they're natural things because we're made in a certain way, to complete ourselves. Anyway, we aren't hurting anyone, are we?

PRIEST: Of course. Often there are requirements of nature, yes. Anyway, outside of regularized marriage, let's say, to do these things is a grave sin, I don't know whether I make myself clear.

PENITENT: All right, it's a sin, but—

PRIEST: It's a sin because it's outside the rules of the Church, because this moment of nature has to be satisfied with the presence of the sacrament. This is the intention of the Church.

PENITENT: But you priests say that even kissing between engaged people is a sin.

PRIEST: No. Who says that?

PENITENT: Some priests have told me that.

PRIEST: No!

PENITENT: Because they say that it can excite and lead to certain—

PRIEST: Well, all right, but it means nothing! The kiss may be accompanied by some emotion, but it's not a problem. Because the kiss is an expression of affection, of sentiment, of love. Do you understand?

PENITENT: I was talking about passionate kisses.

PRIEST: Yes, yes, I see. Well, do you intend to confess, or have you come just to ask for some explanations, some advice? Do you want absolution or don't you?

PENITENT: If you can give me it.

PRIEST: You aren't living with that man yet?

PENITENT: I intend to live with him. On the other hand, being Catholic, I don't want to remain outside the Church.

PRIEST: If you go to live with him, it doesn't mean that you leave the Church. You'll be living in sin, but in the end it's the Lord who judges intentions, not acts, and that's what counts. There must be a good intention, do you see?

PENITENT: Yes, I see. May I come back sometime? What's your name, Father?

PRIEST: M———.

PENITENT: I can come back to you after a few months and see what I've decided.

PRIEST: Yes. I celebrate mass here between nine and nine-thirty. At this time I'm always here.

PENITENT: All right, Father. Thank you.

CHURCH OF THE SACRO CUORE DE GESU, ROME

PRIEST: Jesus Christ be praised.

PENITENT: May He always be praised.

PRIEST: How long is it since you confessed?

PRIEST: Oh . . . about three years.

PRIEST: Why so long? Have you failed to go to mass?

PENITENT: No, I find myself in a special situation.

PRIEST: That's a very good reason for drawing closer to God. Have you failed to attend mass?

PENITENT: No, no, that's not the problem. The problem is that I'm not married or engaged, and now I've gotten older and my physiological and affective needs have become so strong that I'm unhappy.

PRIEST: Are you living with some man?

PENITENT: No, not yet. That's the thing.

PRIEST: And have you done wrong with him?

PENITENT: How's that?

PRIEST: Have you been with him? Have you sinned with him?

PENITENT: Well, now, there is a man that I could be interested in.

PRIEST: But have you done wrong with him or haven't you?

PENITENT: Well, yes.

PRIEST: And how many times a week?

PENITENT: I don't know, I haven't known him long. I've more or less decided to enter into a relationship with this man, but he can't marry me.

PRIEST: Just tell me about your sins, because after all, this is a confession.

PENITENT: I know, but you could give me some advice, couldn't you?

PRIEST: Well, first one has to know how things stand. Have you sinned with him or haven't you?

PENITENT: But I don't feel that it's a sin. I feel that it's a natural thing, when one has gotten to this age.

PRIEST: Then let's say that the natural soul must live in God and with God.

PENITENT: Yes, all right, but there's a physiological need . . . so, what am I to do? Is it better, then, for a person to sin on her own?

PRIEST: But, madam, have you sinned with him or haven't you? So I can know . . . since you must confess. You've come to confess your sins, haven't you?

PENITENT: Well, yes.

PRIEST: Well, then, have you sinned with him or not?

PENITENT: If I say that I haven't sinned but that I intend to do so?

PRIEST: You tell me that . . . eh, no, let's confess what's been done. The first thing you must do is to put your conscience in order, and then we'll see what the problem is, and whether it can be solved. In the meantime, however, set your conscience in order.

PENITENT: All right, but if I intend to start a relationship after?

PRIEST: All right, but first you must tell me whether you've sinned or not.

PENITENT: I see. All right, I have sinned, yes.

PRIEST: And about how many times, roughly?

PENITENT: I don't know. I didn't count them!

PRIEST: But you should have.

PENITENT: I should have counted?

PRIEST: Yes, yes, of course . . . roughly. When you come to confession you have to say how many times. But what kind of ideas do you have about confession? I really don't know.

PENITENT: Father, you're speaking too low, I can't understand.

PRIEST: Confession doesn't just call for the type of sin, when it's a question of chastity, but also the number of times, just as for any other sin.

PENITENT: Why?

PRIEST: Because it helps the confessor to establish the degree of sin, that's why. Have you failed to go to mass?

PENITENT: No, I go every Sunday.

PRIEST: Have you blasphemed?

PENITENT: No, no.

PRIEST: Well, then, have you sinned alone? How many times alone?

PENITENT: No, it's not a question of sinning alone. That problem will come up if I don't . . . if I don't go with this man. In fact, I'd like to know from you which is best.

PRIEST: You can't marry him?

PENITENT: No, because he's legally separated.

PRIEST: Separated?

PENITENT: Yes.

PRIEST: Well, then look for another man!

PENITENT: I can't find one.

PRIEST: Well, then let's see. The only thing is to strengthen one's weakness through the grace of God, with confession and Communion. Do you think you can do this alone? No one can. How can you possibly do it if you only take Communion once every two years? Do you understand? You can't succeed in that way. At least a little will power is needed.

PENITENT: And so I must be unhappy?

PRIEST: Why should you be unhappy?

PENITENT: Because I am.

PRIEST: But chastity brings balance.

PENITENT: No. As a rule, it brings unbalance.

PRIEST: That's what you think. If you use your imagination too much, of course, it does. Just as a man who thinks that he's sick, even if he isn't, ends up by becoming sick.

PENITENT: But—

PRIEST: Now, you must lead your body back again. But you still haven't told me whether it's a sickness or not.

PENITENT: No, I'm not sick!

PRIEST: Well, then, it's a question of will power, madam.

PENITENT: It's not a question of that. It's like being hungry, it's a natural physiological need.

PRIEST: It is not natural. Well, it is and it isn't. This natural need exists, of course, but will power with the aid of grace can overcome it.

PENITENT: All right, then, I'll try to be strong.

PRIEST: [*Inaudible*]

PENITENT: I can't hear anything, Father.

PRIEST: I advise you to use all the will power you can. That way, at least I can absolve you. It may be that you'll fall again, but at least you have the desire. You must consider this to be a sinful situation.

PENITENT: All right.

PRIEST: Well, then, repent as much as you can, I absolve you. You will do penance whenever you can, and receive Communion. Then ... continue, because you can't do without this. But, young lady, you must try to dominate yourself. I know I am asking you to make an effort, but—

PENITENT: All right, Father.

*Some extracts from other conversations in which the priest adopted a more broad-minded attitude.*

CHURCH OF SANT 'AGOSTINO, BOLZANO

PENITENT: Father, my position is very difficult, and it's getting more and more impossible. I've been a widow for three years and I have lived them with the greatest dignity, but I have been mortifying my senses all that time. Now, I can't stand it any more.

PRIEST: You can always remarry.

PENITENT: It's not that easy! I'm forty, I have habits I can't change now. I don't think I'll ever find a suitable man, it's almost impossible.

PRIEST: Have you sinned on your own during this time?

PENITENT: I don't know what you mean, Father.

PRIEST: I mean, have you brought about sexual excitement by using your imagination, touching your sex with your fingers and so on?

PENITENT: I think it's natural for that to happen, accustomed as I was, during marriage, to regular satisfaction of the senses.

PRIEST: Not natural, exactly. I'd say normal. You see, I can understand you very well because we priests, too, are under a similar strain. I imagine that when you take a bath and see your naked body reflected in the mirror, you feel the burden of not being able to give love to that body. And you must feel very excited and a desire to arrive at orgasm. Isn't that the way it is?

PENITENT: Well, yes, a bit.

PRIEST: In these cases, to caress oneself, to touch oneself knowingly, thinking about the male organ maybe or at any rate about male contact, is not a very grave sin. It is always better to confess it, to unburden oneself with the confessor, but it is not really indispensable. Do you understand, madam?

PENITENT: Yes, Father. But if I were to have relations with a man toward whom I feel a certain amount of affection with whom I can never marry, will I lose the right to absolution? It's more natural for me to do these things with a man rather than alone, isn't it?

PRIEST: Is he married?

PENITENT: Separated for over ten years.

PRIEST: The problem is more complex because you end up committing adultery. He's still married, even though separated. He's still the husband of another woman, do you see?

PENITENT: Well, then, what am I to do? If I decide to stay with him do I lose the right to remain within the Church?

PRIEST: No, you don't lose it, but many confessors would not give you absolution.

PENITENT: And would you give it to me?

PRIEST: I ought to advise you against entering into such a relationship, and I ought to point out to you all the dangers you are likely to encounter. But, if you were to decide to enter the relationship just the same, and you felt at peace with your conscience, I would try to put myself in your place and I'd give you absolution.

BARI CATHEDRAL

PRIEST: Your widowed state doesn't prevent you from thinking of marriage. Or is there some impediment?

PENITENT: I have two children, and so I don't want another marriage, at least for the moment. The fact is, there's . . . I'm very fond of a person. Is it a grave sin if I have a relationship like that, without legal bonds?

PRIEST: Certainly, my dear child, you will commit a grave sin. You must not even entertain the idea. But has there already been something between you?

PENITENT: No, no.

PRIEST: Well, then, continue that way. Keep away from that person so you won't be tempted. Do you understand?

PENITENT: The fact is that I feel young and alive.

PRIEST: But, my child, you have two children you love. Devote your energies to them and leave your senses alone.

PENITENT: But the senses exist! I certainly don't want to neglect my children. Indeed, I'm giving up marriage so as not to give them a father they might not like. This doesn't mean that I can't find a bit of affection and love as best I can. I'm fortunate to have a man I'm fond of and who attracts me, and he's fond of me.

PRIEST: No, my child, you are free to do as you like, but I cannot ... I will never be able to advise this nor give you absolution if you have such an intention, do you understand?

PENITENT: All right, Father. That means that I'll have to consider myself outside the Church, because I don't believe that you can condemn a person who's still young and vital to a life of continuous self-repression, constant mortification of the senses and humiliation toward herself.

PRIEST: Look, my child, you are adopting a mistaken attitude due to resentment. It isn't the Church that rejects you if you behave in a certain way, it's *you* who finish outside the Church of your own accord. However, the confessor must not be a rigid applier of rules. You think about what we've said to each other today, weigh your situation carefully, examine your will power, your ability to react to the natural stimuli of sex, and then come back to me. We'll discuss it again. You'll see, we'll find a solution all right.

PENITENT: To go by experience, I don't think there are any solutions besides the one I'm thinking about.

PRIEST: Never mind, we'll see. If that is really the only solution, well ... we'll take it into consideration, shall we?

## CONCLUSION: A LIFE SENTENCE

Only thirty-six of the priests understood the distressing nature of the problem and agreed that the woman should do as her conscience suggests. But, having made this concession, they wash their hands of the matter. The penitent is not to account to them, but directly to God. The other priests barely give any consideration to the problem. They insist that chastity does not cause psychophysical reactions, but rather that it gives them balance.

# V

## THE FAMILY IS NO LONGER A "RABBIT WARREN"

St. AUGUSTINE wrote: "Love your wives, but love them chastely. Practice the carnal act only in the measure necessary for the conception of children. If it happens that you do not want to have children, you must, even though with reluctance, abstain from it."

For centuries Catholic morality has linked the concept of sexuality with the act of procreation. Today, times have changed profoundly. An unlimited increase in the population may well destroy the world.

What is the stand taken by the priests toward married people who no longer want to consider the family as a "rabbit warren"? On this theme we recorded 105 conversations, subdivided here into three categories. The first includes conversations with priests who admit the use of contraceptives or the possibility of the seed's being dispersed at the end of the sexual act. The second consists of conversations with priests who don't consider these acts a sin if one of the couple is forced by the attitude of his or her partner. The third concerns conversations with priests who continue to consider the sexual act exclusively for procreation.

*In 27 of the 105 conversations recorded, the priest said that it*

135

*was all right for the husband and wife to act in such a way that the sexual act might not arrive at procreation. The full text of the most representative conversations follows.*

### CHURCH OF SANT' IGNAZIO, ROME

PRIEST: How long has it been since you confessed?

PENITENT: I don't remember. The fact is, Father, that I'm married, and neither my husband nor I wish to have any more children.

PRIEST: I don't understand this statement.

PENITENT: Since we already have two children, we don't want to have any more.

PRIEST: But why not?

PENITENT: You see, we both work; if others were to come, there'd be a lot of problems. So, we—

PRIEST: Listen, madam, what is it you do to avoid having children? Do you interrupt coitus?

PENITENT: Yes.

PRIEST: Does he wear something?

PENITENT: Well, one or the other.

PRIEST: Madam, do try to dissuade him from using artificial things, because they're always dangerous to your health. A woman's womb is a very delicate thing. God has provided us with powerful biological principles for defense against bacteria, but with a foreign body you're always in danger, do you understand, madam? When people carry out an operation, they use all sorts of aseptic care to avoid infection. Now, a foreign body is always a danger to your health, whereas the natural act—

PENITENT: Yes, but I mean—

PRIEST: If, then, he interrupts of his own accord, you should let him do it. You must not molest him, annoy him, or tease him.

PENITENT: But is it a sin? I mean, am I outside the Church or—

PRIEST: No, no. You cannot deny your husband your chaste affection. If he, then—of his own accord, thinking to do right, in good faith—does that, you let him do it.

PENITENT: But we're both agreed on this so as not to have children.

PRIEST: Yes, yes, but you must not deny your chaste affection. And if, sometimes, you take the initiative, you take it because you don't intend to lead up to this thing. You intend only to have with him that affection that it's right to have, and not neglect him, not be absent in this regard, do you understand? So, in seeking tenderness toward your husband, you are seeking that which is your right, and your duty, too. So, you may feel tranquil for your part. But, of course, dear lady—

PENITENT: Well, then, I can take the pill?

PRIEST: I advise against that, madam.

PENITENT: For a medical reason, or for a religious one?

PRIEST: Moral and also medical. Listen, madam, if the Pope has decided the way he has after hearing all possible advice from the doctors, it hasn't been merely for ... And anyway, the press ... Just today I read in the paper that in America the government has said, "Those who want to take the pill can take it, but at their own risk." In England, officially, quite apart from the many unofficial cases, twenty women died in one year as a result of the pill.

PENITENT: So, then, the best method is still the traditional one of interrupting.

PRIEST: Well, leave it to your husband to do whatever he thinks best, eh?

PENITENT: But I want to know this. I don't—

PRIEST: You don't commit a sin if you go with him, even when you know he's doing that. Do you see, madam?

PENITENT: All right, thanks.

PRIEST: Yes, my dear child, try to remain in peace with the Lord. My sister, who is the mother superior of an institute for polio patients, has told me that there is a nine-year-old orphan, sick with polio, who has been adopted by a lawyer in Bologna who already has five children of his own, of which the youngest is eighteen months old. The wife is thirty-four and has no maid. They've adopted this child and what's more they've adopted a three-year-old girl from India. And the Lord will not fail to bless. And my own mother, I'm the oldest of nine children, adopted a child that was only six days old, and then she took a girl of fourteen. So, dear lady, try, to love your husband respectfully. And if you have your youth and health, give the serene fruit of your youth to the Lord. I understand that there can be reasons, and good ones, that make you feel you don't want more children, but do have in your hearts this feeling of trust and generosity toward the Lord.

PENITENT: Yes, all right.

PRIEST: That's it. Nothing else, madam?

PENITENT: No.

PRIEST: Well, dear lady, you must not hold back in your tender relations with your husband for fear he will then arrive at that act of interruption, because otherwise your conjugal relations will cool, and the man feels himself isolated. He feels his wife is far from him and so he gets the ideas in his head and thinks about other things. On the other hand, when a man finds affection in his dear wife, serene affection and comfort, then it's quite another thing. You must help him to raise himself up, and to lend himself increasingly to those holy bonds that God has established. The children must flourish in a truly good environment. Love each other, don't ever mortify each other, much or little, in front of your children. This will help you a lot in bringing them up to be serene and respectful, affectionate, grateful, docile toward you. All right?

PENITENT: Yes, thank you.

PRIEST: Nothing else, madam?

PENITENT: No.

PRIEST: Say three Hail Marys.

CHURCH OF SAN BABILA, MILAN

PRIEST: May Jesus Christ be praised.

PENITENT: May He always be praised.

PRIEST: How long has it been since you confessed?

PENITENT: Over four months.

PRIEST: Four months? Then you didn't do your Easter duties, did you?

PENITENT: No. You see, the thing is that I have a special problem. My wife and I don't want to have any more children. We already have two, so we see to it that we don't have any more.

PRIEST: Ah, and how is that?

PENITENT: Well, sometimes she takes the pill, and sometimes I interrupt the act before . . .

PRIEST: That's not in line with God's law, though.

PENITENT: Well, I haven't been to confession any more just for that very reason. Because I'm afraid of being told that I'm not a good Christian any more. But, after all, what am I to do? We're still young, it's not that we can abstain from sexual relations!

PRIEST: No, of course not. Have you other valid reasons for not wanting children? Two, after all, is not such a large number.

PENITENT: I don't think it's a question of the number. I think that a person ought to have a child when he feels psychologically ready to have one. Otherwise, it's not a good thing, it's not responsible. Don't you agree?

PRIEST: Look, you must understand that the Church has its morality according to which the sexual act must carry with it the intention of procreation. However, one must admit that there may be very valid reasons for modifying this criterion . . . case by case, do you understand? You must examine your conscience and decide whether the way you're acting permits it, you may carry on in the same way, do you understand?

PENITENT: Then I'm not sinning?

PRIEST: It is a sin as far as sin goes. Does your wife agree to this?

PENITENT: Certainly.

PRIEST: I advise you, however, not to let her use the pill unless it has been prescribed by a doctor. It could be dangerous for her health, and thus, to use it would be a sin because a Christian is duty bound to concern himself with his health, which is a gift of God.

PENITENT: And if I withdraw from her before I ejaculate?

PRIEST: It's still dispersion of the seed. You must decide for yourself according to your conscience. Do you understand?

PENITENT: But must I confess it each time?

PRIEST: Well, yes. I mean, no. No, it's not necessary. Pray to God to help you arrive at the right decision.

PENITENT: Thank you, Father. There's something else I'd like to know. Would it be a grave sin to have an abortion?

PRIEST: It's a crime. Not only for the Church, but also for the law. Why? Do you have such intentions, perhaps?

PENITENT: No, no, I was just asking to find out.

PRIEST: Look, if you're hiding something from me, I shan't find it out, but God sees all and the absolution I give you will have no value whatsoever. Do you understand?

PENITENT: Yes, yes.

PRIEST: All right. Have you anything else to confess?

PENITENT: No, I don't think so.

PRIEST: Have you been to mass every Sunday?

PENITENT: Sometimes I've missed.

PRIEST: Try not to miss going to mass. Have you always behaved well with your friends and colleagues at work?

PENITENT: Yes.

PRIEST: Good. Say three Our Fathers for penance.

CHURCH OF SAN MARCELLO AL CORSO, ROME

PRIEST: May Jesus Christ be praised.

PENITENT: May He always be praised.

PRIEST: How long is it since you confessed?

PENITENT: A few months.

PRIEST: What have you done?

PENITENT: Father, I'm married and I have a problem. We already have four children and we don't want to have any more. So I take the pill, and I want to know if it's a sin.

PRIEST: It's a very big problem, my sister. You know very well the pill has a dual aspect—physical, let's say a hygienic-health one which you must discuss with your doctor, and moral, which you must consider within your own heart, before God. You must look at these things in a responsible way. We must realize that we have to account to God. Abstaining from having children in this way, even if it's necessary for the peace of the family, must be decided by you in your secret heart, listening to what your conscience suggests to you, before God. You see, you're the one who's in trouble, in the sense that you're a wife and mother. You don't want to have any more children and on the other hand you can't go on like that. You yourself must solve your problem, with simplicity before God, to see whether you're thinking of yourself or whether you really have valid justification. Do you understand?

PENITENT: So, then, if I continue in the same way do I have to confess every time?

PRIEST: Do it before God. If you feel tranquil, there's no need for you to confess it.

PENITENT: That's just it. I wanted—

PRIEST: As long as this state of things continues, do it before God.

PENITENT: If not, is there some other system that you can advise?

PRIEST: Look, I don't know exactly what ... A doctor can advise you better in these things. The important thing is for you not to be an egotist, not deny your sacrament. Sometimes there are people who are able to have children but find excuses for not having them because they're lazy, because—

PENITENT: Well, it's not that I can't have them, I can.

PRIEST: Physically you can have them. But are you in a condition to accept another child morally? Does your family situation make it possible? As you see, it's a strictly personal matter for you to judge for yourself. I don't know whether you have understood.

PENITENT: Yes, yes, I see.

PRIEST: And then, what else do you recall?

PENITENT: Nothing else.

PRIEST: Let us place the whole of our lives at God's feet, let us try to sincerely love Him. Draw near to Him, hear His voice that speaks to us. He knows that we wish to love Him. For penance, seven Hail Marys to Our Lady, seven Glorias to Jesus.

*The following are extracts from other conversations in which the priest shows himself to be understanding.*

CHURCH OF SAN GIUSEPPE, AGRIGENTO

PENITENT: Father, my wife doesn't want to have any more children. I find myself forced to behave ...

PRIEST: ... to behave unlike a good Catholic, in short.

PENITENT: To tell the truth, I can't understand either why we should bring children into the world if we don't feel the need for it inside ourselves and if all kinds of difficulties would result.

PRIEST: Because God wishes it, my son. God has not given us testicles and vaginas for us to get pleasure out of them, but to reproduce the species. The pleasure, in short, is a stimulus to reproduction. However, those who don't want to load themselves down with a mass of children are not altogether in the wrong either. How many do you have?

PENITENT: Two.

PRIEST: Well, that's not many. You could have more!

PENITENT: But we feel that's the right number to make sure that they're well brought up and have a good education. And then, excuse me, with the world threatened by overpopulation and what not, don't you think it's ironic for the Church to go on preaching that we should have as many children as possible? It's these stands on the Church's part that often puzzle me and even make me doubt my faith.

PRIEST: The Church is modifying its stand. In fact, in recent times, it has become tolerant and benevolent even toward those married couples who don't think of intercourse just as a procreative event and nothing more.

PENITENT: But it's not a question of showing itself to be tolerant and benevolent. I think it would be more responsible if it were to advise couples to limit the number of births to a maximum so that—

PRIEST: The Church will arrive at this, never fear!

PENITENT: As long as it doesn't arrive too late!

PRIEST: The Church is inspired by God. Leave it to God! In a case like yours it's the conscience that counts. If you think it's right to do this, if you don't feel uneasy about it, it means you may continue tranquilly because God approves. Do you understand?


CHURCH OF SANT 'ANTONIO, CHIANCIANO

PRIEST: What reason do you have for not wanting to have children?

PENITENT: None. We already have four and we don't want any more, that's all.

PRIEST: You take it [the pill] to avoid disagreement with your husband—do so. In that case, you're all right. If anything, it will be your husband who isn't altogether all right.

PENITENT: But, I'm in agreement too. It's not that my husband is forcing me to take the pill.

PRIEST: Do you know that there are periods in which you can have intercourse without procreative consequences?

PENITENT: Of course. But it's not a question of this period or that. Our third child was conceived during a period in which, according to the rhythm method, I was supposed to be infertile.

PRIEST: Do as you think then.

PENITENT: Can I go on taking the pill?

PRIEST: Continue as you have been doing with the intention of preserving conjugal love.


## BLAME THE OTHER SPOUSE

*In 46 of the 105 conversations taped, the priest falls back on a handy compromise solution: he grants that one partner can carry out the sexual act without the danger of procreation, as long as the responsibility for the decision is that of the other partner.*

CHURCH OF SAN BARTOLOMMEO, BERGAMO

PRIEST: Has it been long since your last confession?
PENITENT: I don't remember.
PRIEST: Roughly?
PENITENT: Four or five months.
PRIEST: What sins have you committed during that time?
PENITENT: Well, Father, I really wanted some advice. My wife and I don't want to have any more children. Especially my wife, since she had a very bad time with the last birth. She's terrified at the idea of having another like that. So I try to

complete the sexual act outside the natural place so as not to run any risks.

PRIEST: It's against the law of God.

PENITENT: That's the point. That's why I haven't been to confession. What must I do then, endanger our marriage? I think my wife would almost hate me if I were to make her pregnant again. Or should we not make love any more and ruin the family just the same?

PRIEST: Don't be so dramatic! There are other ways that are permitted by the Church. For instance, you can have relations on the days your wife is infertile—the rhythm method.

PENITENT: Sure, but it doesn't offer an absolute guarantee.

PRIEST: Not to those who apply it improperly. But for those who understand it thoroughly it's absolutely sure.

PENITENT: There are lots of children in the world born just because of the rhythm method!

PRIEST: Out of ignorance. Why is it that people make their calculations according to the days and menstrual intervals instead of . . . Do you know what should be used for calculation?

PENITENT: The vaginal temperature.

PRIEST: Ah! There you are. You know! When your wife has her menstrual period, you must measure the temperature of the vagina with a thermometer. If the thermometer shows a temperature different from the normal, then you can make an exact calculation. If, on the other hand, there is no change in temperature, it means that there's not a real and proper menstruation and thus all calculations. . . In short, much more prudence is needed. Do you understand?

PENITENT: Well, Father, it's something I did know, but also it's a thing I'll never do. I feel it's humiliating for a woman and embarrassing for me too. But you must explain something to me. I use the thermometer on my wife, I do the calculation, and then I do the sexual act with her when I'm sure that there won't be any consequences, right? What difference is there, then, if she takes the pill, or if I withdraw from her before I feel pleasure and thus before ejaculating the seed? Aren't we sure in all three cases that the act won't have consequences and that it doesn't therefore, matter or have procreation as its aim? I don't understand, therefore, why one thing is all right and the other not.

PRIEST: The law of God rules that the act must take place in the natural way, without pills—which are an intervention from outside—and without interruption. If there are natural conditions, like cycles of sterility, which prevent procreation . . . these are, in fact, natural things not created by the will of man.

PENITENT: Well, that's open to discussion. Because if I wait until those very days in which I *know* that my wife is infertile, there's just the same definite will on my part, isn't there? Anyway, Father, I want to know since my wife doesn't want to have any more children, am I committing a sin in backing her up in this desire of hers?

PRIEST: You're not committing a sin on condition that you're behaving in this way just so as not to disturb your wife. In short, you submit to the decision, you are not a participant in it.

PENITENT: I can't say that because at the bottom I'm convinced that my wife is right and that it isn't just to bring children into the world in obedience to a law that may be altered by the Church in a few years' time.

PRIEST: No, the Church will never alter this law.

PENITENT: It seems a bit risky to say that, Father, since there was a time in which it looked as if the Pope were going to say that the use of the pill was permissible. Only at the last minute, and maybe for reasons that were more medical than moral, he drew back. So—

PRIEST: But right now it's this way, and every good Catholic must do as the Sovereign Pontiff has ruled. In any case, I repeat—you behave as your wife suggests, but leave the responsibility for the decision to her. That is, you do what you're doing so as to avoid useless and harmful complications in your family situation. You're forced into it by things beyond your control. So you're not committing a sin.

PENITENT: All right. Thank you Father.

PRIEST: You're welcome.

*In some instances, the priest's comments are not entirely coherent. The breaks in the comments below are not omissions, but silences.*

## CHURCH OF SAN CARLO, GENOA

PENITENT: Since we've already got a child, we don't want to have another.

PRIEST: I know. First of all, one must place oneself in God's hands, because after all, it is God who gives us what He wants.

PENITENT: But I take the pill.

PRIEST: Yes, that's a bit . . . There are the days that are infertile.

PENITENT: I know, but that's always very relative.

PRIEST: On the other hand, one must allow some latitude in these things. After all, we can't go directly against that which God asks.

PENITENT: But can I go on taking the pill?

PRIEST: The pill is already something that goes directly against the what-you-call-it. And then, on the other hand, it seems it's not so efficient and can also cause harm. Because medicines always have a good side and a—

PENITENT: Do I have to confess every time I take it?

PRIEST: This would be necessary, yes. But then, on the other hand, I think that to abuse this stuff is always harmful. It may have its effect and prevent conception, that's true, but it can always lead to . . . That's violent stuff! In the end it brings about a lack of balance and can have bad consequences if repeated over and over. Medicine should be taken when one is ill, because it's indispensable, but medicine at bottom is always a poison, always.

PENITENT: Well, then, it is better that he doesn't finish the act.

PRIEST: I'd say that it was a bit.

PENITENT: But what difference is there between the pill and that?

PRIEST: Both of them are not permissible in themselves, because the matrimonial act must be an act that leads to the possibility of conception. There must not be anything that impedes it. Now, there are certain days each month that . . . thing doesn't usually happen. And so, during those days, one may tranquilly perform the act.

PENITENT: All right, but what about the other days?

PRIEST: One must do everything possible to abstain the other days. Of course, it is a bit of a sacrifice. But on the other hand, if we make this sacrifice, I'm sure that the Lord realizes it and knows how much it costs us. It's painful, I know that.

PENITENT: You must realize, Father, that my husband isn't the kind to stand idly by for five or six days. And then, I'm afraid he'll go with another woman.

PRIEST: Yes, I understand. Between the two things, it's better for him to withdraw at the right moment, but without your direct cooperation.

PENITENT: What does that mean? I mean, what am I to do?

PRIEST: Well, allowing him to withdraw because it's a thing that may prevent . . . that, yes. But cooperating so that he withdraws would be a direct action.

PENITENT: In what way? I don't understand.

PRIEST: In the sense that . . . cooperating in such a way that, if he wishes to, he may withdraw.

PENITENT: All right, but actually I don't want a child at present either, do you understand?

PRIEST: Yes, I do. But one child is rather little, and so place yourself in God's hands. When we try to act virtuously, we can be certain that Our Lord will help us.

PENITENT: All right.

PRIEST: We think a bit too much about our human burden.

But it's necessary that we carry it. This is not a reproach, because it's more or less the same for everyone. We all think of our burdens and we'd like to have more freedom to amuse ourselves. That's only human.

PENITENT: Anyway, can I take Communion when there are these things?

PRIEST: If there are these things, you really can't. Let's put it this way—if he were to withdraw without your doing something positive, leaving it to him to do, then you would not be sinning because it would not be full cooperation. There you are, eh!

PENITENT: I see.

PRIEST: Yes, because otherwise it would be direct cooperation in the thing. And this decision is human, because you can't refuse his intentions. He could then turn elsewhere, and this would be a greater evil in the sense that it would be a rift in the unity of the family, wouldn't it?

PENITENT: Yes.

PRIEST: And between the two evils, it's better to choose the lesser one, but trying not to cooperate actively, that is, to let him do it.

PENITENT: All right. Thank you, Father.

PRIEST: You must have courage. Besides, you must place yourself in God's hands. After all, we have to go to Him in the end because our life has a termination, and if we try to pass this life as Our Lord asks us to we will have an eternal life of true happiness. Think about this a little. Let us try to do our duty. If it's possible to stay away from each other, so much the better. And if not, try to do things without medicines, because medicines do harm in other parts. Violent stuff always brings disasters.

PENITENT: I'll try to talk to my husband and see whether—

PRIEST: You must try to persuade him. Tell him, "Look, let's be good for two or three evenings."

PENITENT: All right. And for penance, Father?

PRIEST: Yes, pray with conviction before God and say three Our Fathers, three Hail Marys, and three Glorias.

CHURCH OF THE SANTISSIME STIMMATE, ROME

PRIEST: How long is it since you confessed?

PENITENT: I don't know, about two months.

PRIEST: What sins have you to tell us about?

PENITENT: Father, I'm married, I have two children, and I don't want to have any more. So relations with my husband are, let's say, not normal, in the sense that he interrupts . . .

PRIEST: . . . the sexual act.

PENITENT: Yes. I want to know whether it's a sin.

PRIEST: It depends. Truly, this is a very serious and very difficult problem. Both you and your husband must become convinced that you have this grace of God in order to live a married life such as God wishes. But, as I say, this often depends on the husband too. Often they don't understand, they see in marriage only a material thing, in which husband and wife unite to live a purely material life.

PENITENT: There's something else. The things they call love play, I do them. I like them. Is this a sin?

PRIEST: No, no. Just as long as you arrive at the complete material act, it isn't a sin. Unfortunately there's the danger that if a person doesn't have this grace of the Lord—and to keep that grace one must not comit sins—it's very difficult to define this "play." There's the danger of not ending up with the act. But anyway, for your own part at least, be passive.

PENITENT: Passive? But I like it too.

PRIEST: When your husband asks you to do the act and you know that he won't do it properly, let each one go his or her own way. Try to advise him. You care for your husband. Make sure that he doesn't have any spiritual illness either, which is the most serious illness, mortal sin. For this reason, as you understand, try as far as possible not to take part in these acts when you know that he won't arrive at the complete act.

PENITENT: But the fact is, he interrupts so as not to have any more children, and I'm in agreement with that. Should I feel guilty or not? In other words, am I outside the Church?

PRIEST: Outside the Church, no. In this sense, you cannot [*inaudible*]

PENITENT: I can't?

PRIEST: You must not give up your husband.

PENITENT: I mustn't give him up?

PRIEST: You must try to do it, if he asks you to. If you're able to convince him not to do it, well . . .

PENITENT: But I want him to do what he's doing, too. That is, the thought of having another child terrifies me. So if I know that he's taking every precaution, the relationship becomes more serene, do you understand?

PENITENT: Yes, yes, I see. For this reason, I say, in those moments you should try not to seek pleasure.

PENITENT: Yes, yes, I do seek it. Perhaps I haven't made myself clear. In other words, I feel all right only when I know that he's going to interrupt before anything happens. Only then can I let myself go completely. Otherwise I can't, since if I know that something might . . . The idea of getting pregnant and all that blocks me, and not only do I fail to feel pleasure, but I can't even do the normal act. Do you understand?

PRIEST: Yes, yes. As I said, it's very difficult for that reason. It's very difficult to set limitations. May God enlighten you, ask this grace of God, to do—

PENITENT: Then I'm not outside the Church?

PRIEST: No, no. Why?

PENITENT: Can I—

PRIEST: You can come. But you must confess when you do these things. Come each time and don't worry. Look, we are weak and God is great and merciful and forgives our weaknesses. As I said, act passively when you know that your husband is going to make love to you and not do it properly. In other acts, touchings, kisses, glances, you can do this quite all right. When, though, your husband asks you to perform the act, then at that time you must act passively.

PENITENT: But why do I have to act passively? I don't understand.

PRIEST: Because if at that moment you're seeking pleasure, and you know that the act will not be done according to the rules of nature, then that's an act against nature.

PENITENT: All right, but I can't prevent myself from feeling pleasure because of that, can I?

PRIEST: Yes, because you're making yourself an accomplice of that sin or of that act that has not been done according to nature.

PENITENT: And so?

PRIEST: As I said, in that act, you must show yourself to be—

PENITENT: No, no, it's not possible, because if I'm passive I get no pleasure. Do you understand? It's not possible to ... to feel pleasure and be passive.

PRIEST: Yes, a passivity up to a certain point. For instance, your husband doesn't do the complete act, you try not to ask for it, and, if you don't ask for it—

PENITENT: But I can't prevent it once you've started to perform the act. How can you prevent it from giving you pleasure?

PRIEST: No, no, you can't prevent it once you've started to perform the act. How can you prevent it from giving you pleasure?

PENITENT: Exactly.

PRIEST: It's useless. But at least don't be the one to take the leading part in the act.

PENITENT: All right. But why? I mean, what responsibility would I have?

PRIEST: You'd have the responsibility of willingly committing a sin, for seeking this sin or that other one which will be a bad act.

PENITENT: And so my responsibility would be graver.

PRIEST: So, when he asks you to do this act, you must act as passively as you can, as much as you can. And then you say, "I have performed this act involuntarily. I didn't really want to, but my husband asked me to and I must do it." You see, if you show yourself to be a slave of your husband, then your husband ...

PENITENT: . . . he becomes responsible?

PRIEST: No, no, it's not that he becomes responsible. If the husband asks for the act, and the wife says to him, "Some other time, some other time," then he thinks that there's no love. He may go out to find another woman.

PENITENT: Exactly. So I have to be the one, sometimes, to take the initiative, to prove to him—

PRIEST: No, to take the initiative, no. You must take the initiative, yes, for . . . no, you mustn't take the initiative there.

PENITENT: Why mustn't I take the initiative?

PRIEST: Because you know you're going to commit an act that's not good, a sin. And for this reason you mustn't take the initiative. You must allow your husband to take you, but when he takes you, you mustn't draw back, because there's the danger that the husband may go and commit another sin outside that's graver, and so it's better—

PENITENT: It's better for us to commit the sin within the family.

PRIEST: Yes.

PENITENT: All right.

PRIEST: This is a very difficult problem, and then another confessor may possibly tell you something else. But think that God is watching us and one must always be tranquil even if one has to weep, isn't that right? The ideal would be for the husband and the wife to be capable of acting correctly. Look, you must realize that the matrimonial side is not the solution of married life. Because if there's the matrimonial act but there's not that love, that affection, that delicacy of the wife toward the husband, that is shown not only in the matrimonial act but is also in daily life, then—

PENITENT: From the husband toward the wife as well, though!

PRIEST: Yes, yes, the same. It's a thing . . .

PENITENT: . . . that's mutual.

PRIEST: Yes, mutual. Then, that's truly a marriage. When the husband, for instance, goes out alone into the city and he has the idea of going with these women of the streets. He thinks, "All right, instead of spending a lot of money here, I'll buy my wife a dress and take her this present." There is delicacy on the part of the husband which increases love and the happiness of the family. The wife must do the same. If she knows that he likes tobacco, wine, cognac, and that he likes coffee at a certain hour, makes a little sacrifice and gives it to him already prepared so that when he arrives he finds it there. These are small things to which no importance is attached but happiness in marriage is in these things. As I said, this is very difficult. One needs very strong grace from God and an equally strong religious training. Maybe the priests have neglected this, have let things slide, and so we've arrived at divorce. Why don't people want to talk about these things? Why? Is there any real preparation of girls and boys for marriage so that they know what it really is? If it is a sacrament of the Church, it must have something spiritual in it. It must be a meeting, a union, to serve God and love Him more strongly. You and your husband must not worry about each other because you have no spiritual guilt, no mortal sin. That is, in the truest sense. You won't be capable of doing it all at once. It depends on your husband as well, doesn't it?

PENITENT: Yes, but the fact is that we don't believe we're doing anything harmful and so—

PRIEST: Doing no harm? The Lord has given us this power, this authority, this strength to make a person, to create a human life, and we use it for another purpose. Well, then, we're abusing that which the Lord has given us, and for this reason it becomes a sin.

PENITENT: All right. Thank you, Father.

PRIEST: Good. Courage, madam, don't worry, always confess. You must be concerned not only for you but also for your husband. When I say this I don't mean that the responsibility is all yours. Both of you are responsible. May your spiritual life be stronger and may there always be spiritual health in your home.

PENITENT: Thanks.

PRIEST: Good. As prayer and penance say two Our Fathers, two Hail Marys, and two Glorias.

*We report below the more interesting extracts from other conversations concerning married people who don't want to have more children. In these, as in the other conversations in this chapter, the priest, with a somewhat singular interpretation of the conjugal relationship, tries to free the partner who is confessing from guilt, at the expense of the absent partner.*

CHURCH OF THE SANTISSIMA ANNUNZIATA, SALERNO

PENITENT: You see, Father, we don't want any more children.

PRIEST: Well, then, follow the Ogino-Knauss system, which is safe if—

PENITENT: Not really.

PRIEST: No, listen to me carefully, my child, it serves. If, in love, there is the ability to sacrifice oneself, this method does not fail. But it does call for a careful calculation in which one can be certain that there is no conception. But don't even consider the possibility of an incomplete act, my child.

PENITENT: Why, is it a sin?

PRIEST: Well, of course it's a sin.

PENITENT: And the use of the pill?

PRIEST: No, no, not that! The Church has never approved it in the most absolute manner.

PENITENT: But once a priest told me that I could take it, under medical supervision.

PRIEST: No, no. I don't know who that priest was, but he acted on his own initiative. These things do harm to the health.

PENITENT: But what must I do then? What am I to say to my husband?

PRIEST: You can be with him when you know that you can't conceive, that's all. This is the only solution that's permitted.

PENITENT: But he wants to do it all the time, that's the only thing. And I'm afraid that if I say no, he'll go with another woman.

PRIEST: Well, then, don't take the initiative. It's a thing that's against the law of nativity. You must not participate actively in an act that is not complete. You can submit to it, yes. All right then, just submit to it.

CHURCH OF THE MADDALENA, ROME

PENITENT: We don't want more children . . .

PRIEST: Does he withdraw so as not to have children? That is, withdraw so as not to leave the sperm . . . so as not to make you pregnant?

PENITENT: He said that I ought to take contraceptive pills.

PRIEST: Ah, I understand . . . contraceptives.

PENITENT: Can I take them?

PRIEST: Oh, goodness, my dear, you decide. Try it. How old are you?

PENITENT: Thirty-six.

PRIEST: You're still young. Have you any children?

PENITENT: Yes, two.

PRIEST: Well, try to do whatever you can. Pretend to take them, maybe.

PENITENT: How's that, pretend to take them? No, because I don't really want to have children either, now. So, I'd like to know whether it's a sin or not.

PRIEST: It's up to you, see what you can do.

PENITENT: But is it a sin to take the pill, or isn't it?

PRIEST: Oh, goodness, sin . . . If one does it for a bad reason, it becomes a sin. Do you understand? Do as you like, anyway, and leave all the responsibility to him.

TEMPIO MONUMENTALE, MODENA

PENITENT: You see, Father, I've been married to a fine woman for five years and we have two children. I'd like to know whether it's a sin to do the sexual act in such a way so as not to have children.

PRIEST: Sin is sin. But do it how, so as not to have children?

PENITENT: Well, Father, it's obvious, isn't it? Not leaving the seed inside the woman. Or letting my wife take the pill.

PRIEST: And where do you want to leave the seed? In the backside? What do you think? You come here and think you can—

PENITENT: But I didn't say that. All one has to do is to withdraw before arriving at completion of the sexual act, that's all.

PRIEST: But these are all sins, and grave ones. And then, the pill . . . Do you know that it can ruin your wife?

PENITENT: If there's medical supervision, I don't think so. And then, it's not me that wants to make her take it, she doesn't want to have any more children at the moment, either.

PRIEST: Ah, you have only two children and you don't want any more. Good. But if it's your wife's fault, you let her get on with it, that's her affair. I don't say that your conscience is completely clear, but you're not in grave sin, either. Anyway, try to dissuade her. If she still insists, pretend that nothing's the matter, so as not to ruin the peace of the family.

PENITENT: It's not like that, to tell the truth. My wife doesn't want to have any more children, and I agree with her completely. We have two—the right number, isn't it? There are other, complementary interests. There's more time to devote to the children we already have. Then there's ourselves as well. We're still young. It's only right that we should want to live with a bit of spare time for ourselves as well. Don't you think so, Father?

PRIEST: Yes, but there are some established laws of God that people must respect.

PENITENT: But the Church recently admitted that the sexual act need not necessarily be understood as an act aimed essentially at procreation.

PRIEST: And so what? All you have to do is to abstain on the days when the woman is . . . that is, there is the danger—

PENITENT: Yes, but—

PRIEST: A woman is fertile only four days in each month, so all that is needed is a sense of responsibility and—

PENITENT: If the four or five days of fertility could be pinned down with absolute certainty, I don't think there'd be any problem for anyone. But instead, as experience has proved, it's just a matter of luck. So it's better not to run risks, interrupting the act at the right moment, isn't it?

PRIEST: If you're the one who takes the initiative in the interruption, you're committing a very grave sin. It's useless for you to insist. On the other hand, if it's your wife who asks you to do it, then, in this case, you may. But leave it up to her, it's her responsibility. In these cases, we priests advise people not to go against the wishes of the other partner so as not to bring family troubles. There's a certain amount of tolerance toward the one who submits to the decision, do you understand?

## CHASTITY OR RHYTHM

*In 32 of the 104 conversations taped, the priest showed himself to be completely intransigent. Two Catholic partners who do not wish to have any more children have only two possibilities: abstain from the sexual act or follow the rhythm method. Any other means or system is grave sin.*

Church of San Giuseppe, Bologna

PRIEST: How long is it since you last confessed?

PENITENT: I don't remember very well.

PRIEST: It doesn't matter. What have you done?

PENITENT: You see, Father, I really want some advice, not to confess. There's a problem that's troubling me and my wife. We don't want to have any more children, seeing that we already have two. So I'm very careful. But I realize that my wife feels uncomfortable, because she's afraid of falling into sin.

PRIEST: What do you mean by saying you're careful?

PENITENT: Well, obviously, I interrupt the act before my orgasm, so that there's no danger.

PRIEST: Ah. I thought that the greatest prudence was abstinence. Don't you think so? If you abstain, you're really safe.

PENITENT: All right, but what has that to do with it? My wife and I are only just over thirty. You surely don't expect us to live like monks from now on!

PRIEST: It's not a question of what I may or may not want. There's a law, a law of God, which established very definite rules—the seed destined for fertilization, destined to create new life, must not be dispersed. It's a crime to disperse it.

PENITENT: But, Father, that's a statement against nature, that not even the Church maintains any more.

PRIEST: Against nature?

PENITENT: Certainly, against nature. On all the days on which the woman is not fertile, and she's not fertile due to a natural fact, isn't the man's seed dispersed? Does it mean, perhaps, that nature, in making woman unfertile, is committing a crime, seeing that man's seed is dispersed?

PRIEST: It always ends up in the woman's womb.

PENITENT: But that's splitting hairs. The fact is that the Church backed these theories when nothing was known about woman's fertile and nonfertile periods, when it was thought that woman was always fertile. Now, the Church is trying to make amends. But many priests are still standing firm on stands like yours, Father, and this brings about a lot of unhappiness to many families. Don't you realize that?

PRIEST: Listen, have you come here to preach to me?

PENITENT: Not at all. I've already told you why I've come here. I sense that my wife feels uncomfortable—she's a very devout Catholic—when I interrupt the sexual act. I wanted to know what arguments you would put forth to explain why two married people should face the choice of having dozens of children or not making love any more. But I see that there aren't any serious arguments.

PRIEST: You're blaspheming. You're saying that God's law is not a serious thing. Do you realize that?

PENITENT: I didn't say that. What I say is that there can't be a law of God which backs that kind of principle. Anyway, the Church recently admitted that the sexual act does not necessarily have procreation as its sole aim. The only thing is that, after having proclaimed this, there was no explanation of the ways in which one could make love without having children. That way there's great confusion and I, with my wife being afraid of sinning, and confessors incapable of explaining to her that to interrupt the act isn't a sin, I find myself in a ridiculous situation, that's all.

PRIEST: Listen, you can chatter as much as you like, but don't expect me to believe that the Church now allows everybody to do just as they please. The Church, at the very most, grants the use of the Ogino-Knauss method. So it's a bit different from what you say!

PENITENT: I don't know what directives you priests are given. I know only that the scientists have said that if we want to avoid the overpopulation of the world and thus the end of the human race, we have to put a stop to the increase of the upside-down pyramid of the world's population. You priests, instead, are doing exactly the opposite. You create every possible difficulty for those who wish to limit the number of their children, intelligently and with wisdom. In other words, you're pushing mankind toward its end.

PRIEST: Listen, my dear fellow, I have no time to waste on these stupidities. Science has been wrong so many times, why should it be right now? Then, there's God who protects man and if God inspires this stand by the Church, it means that it's well done. Have you anything else to say?

PENITENT: No. Thanks.

CHURCH OF SANTA MARIA DEL POPOLO, ROME

PRIEST: How long is it since you confessed?

PENITENT: Several years.

PRIEST: Did you celebrate Easter last year?

PENITENT: No, I didn't go to confession because I'm married, I have three children, and since we don't want to have any more, I've taken the pill, even before the Pope's encyclical forbade it. A priest had told me that I could. So I took it, and that's the reason why I haven't been to confession.

PRIEST: Do you take it often?

PENITENT: Yes, regularly.

PRIEST: Still?

PENITENT: Yes, because I have three children and no intention of having a fourth.

PRIEST: It's dangerous.

PENITENT: I do it under medical supervision.

PRIEST: But, if a thing isn't permissible, medical supervision can't make it permissible. It's still forbidden.

PENITENT: Forbidden in what sense?

PRIEST: The Pope has said no, and so—

PENITENT: The Pope said according to one's conscience.

PRIEST: No, he didn't say according to one's conscience. The pill is forbidden. In addition to the Pope's prohibition, there's also the danger to your health.

PENITENT: But that confessor who gave me permission—

PRIEST: Maybe before, but not now, because the Pope has said no, and it's absolutely no.

PENITENT: So what methods should one use?

PRIEST: When one has embraced the matrimonial state, it is to accept children and do things in the regular manner.

PENITENT: I can't. Either I don't make love with my husband or we get more children.

PRIEST: No, no. Try to behave as you should. Follow what the Church tells you to save your soul.

PENITENT: And then, if we get more children? I don't understand.

PRIEST: Well, God will provide. If you behave well, God sees this.

PENITENT: I know that, but, for instance—

PRIEST: No, this thing that you say, "We don't want any more children," that's not a good thing.

PENITENT: No, because I already have three. And I work, I can't bring them up properly. If I had a fourth it would be—

PRIEST: You see, madam, where children are concerned, you must be capable also of mortification.

PENITENT: What does "multiplication" mean?

PRIEST: No, not "multiplication," "mortification."

PENITENT: But do I commit a sin if my husband and I don't complete the act?

PRIEST: Ah, yes, madam. That point doesn't change.

PENITENT: I know, but then, if the pill is forbidden—

PRIEST: The pill is forbidden because the Pope says no. There's nothing to be done about it. These are all actions against marriage. You understand?

PENITENT: But we already have three children!

PRIEST: We were six children, but we always managed.

PENITENT: Yes, but it used to be different. Probably your mother didn't work away from home, as I do.

PRIEST: But the others worked too.

PENITENT: In any case, if I take the pill, do I have to go to confession every time?

PRIEST: Of course.

PENITENT: I understand.

PRIEST: But . . . listen to me, don't do it.

PENITENT: I don't want to drive my husband away from me.

PRIEST: Your husband will not turn away from you, if you behave as a good Christin.

PENITENT: Since I'm afraid that another child may come, our relations would become neurotic.

PRIEST: But don't be afraid, with persuasion everything will be all right.

PENITENT: It's not a question of persuasion!

PRIEST: You do as I say—with persuasion. Recommend yourself to Our Lord, to Our Lady. Do you understand? Try to behave well.

PENITENT: All right, I'll try.

PRIEST: Make a promise. You'll be happier.

PENITENT: I'll talk to my husband about it, anyway, because I can't decide on my own. I don't know whether he feels like practicing abstinence.

PRIEST: Do your very best, madam, eh? To do things like a good Christian?

PENITENT: All right.

PRIEST: Listen to me. I speak for your own good and for the good of your soul. Try to behave well because God helps those who behave well. Do you understand? Have you committed any other sins?

PENITENT: No.

PRIEST: Say three Our Fathers, three Hail Marys, and three Glorias to Our Lady.

## CONCLUSION: THE EASIEST WAY OUT

The majority of the priests consulted realize that the concept of the family as a "rabbit warren" is no longer valid in today's social situation, and that it is an expression of social immaturity. But these same priests are unable to forget that until the recent past it was an expression of Christianity. For this reason, they chose the easiest (but also the least convincing) way out: the recourse to expedients and compromise.

# VI

## SEPARATED PERSONS

THE PROBLEM we put to 123 priests, in this series of conversations, is one of the saddest: Can a married person who is separated or divorced start life again with another partner, or is he or she condemned to pass the remaining years in loneliness and chastity?

All the priests questioned continue to view sacramental marriage as valid, even if it has broken up without the slightest chance of mending. The only solution permitted the separated partner is a life of faithfulness to the broken bond and thus of absolute chastity. Twenty-one priests, however, out of the 123 heard, granted absolution, in spite of the fact that the penitent states that he or she has built up a new and valid relationship and isn't prepared to give it up. The other 102 declared that the separated or divorced partner who has formed a new relationship is in grave sin and, naturally, denied absolution to them.

## SEPARATION MEANS CONDEMNED FOR LIFE

CHURCH OF SANT' ANTONIO DA PADOVA, PALERMO

PRIEST: Has it been a long time since you confessed?

PENITENT: Well, yes. You see, Father, I'm in a difficult situation and I think I have to consider myself outside the Church. So I didn't bother to confess or receive Communion. Then, today, I realized that so many things have changed in the Church, who knows, there may be greater understanding for cases like mine too.

PRIEST: What is your case?

PENITENT: I'm married, separated from my husband, and I have a relationship with another man.

PRIEST: Ah! How could you hope to find understanding for such a gravely sinful situation!

PENITENT: Well, I hoped—

PRIEST: Why did you separate from your husband?

PENITENT: We didn't get along. You know, Father, before living together, one doesn't notice a lot of things, a lot of faults aren't obvious. And then, we got married without having premarital relations and afterward it was a disaster.

PRIEST: You mean, you didn't get along with him even in bed?

PENITENT: There was lack of understanding there too.

PRIEST: Did he behave in a bestial way? Did he force you to do filthy things?

PENITENT: No, no, at least I don't think so. What do you mean by filthy things?

PRIEST: I meant, did he force you to do things that embarrassed or disgusted you? I don't know, kissing you . . . even . . . even your sex?

PENITENT: Immediately after marriage, I felt embarrassed about doing certain things, but not because they seemed filthy

... because we didn't get on, we didn't have the same sort of feelings, that's all. I do the same things with naturalness, love, and pleasure with the man with whom I have a relationship now.

PRIEST: That's bad, very bad. You ought not to have given up, you ought not to accept the failure with your husband with resignation. In the eyes of the Church and Jesus Christ you remain tied to him for the rest of your life. You see, my child, he may have taken you in the wrong way. Now, you must forget about the other man and start all over again with your husband—right from the start, do you understand? Both of you have more experience now, and you'll see that, certainly.

PENITENT: But he too has another relationship now! Even supposing I wanted to, he probably wouldn't agree. We're much better as we are, Father, believe me.

PRIEST: And so, my child, you are both committing sin, and when one is sinning, life holds nothing but bitterness and disillusion.

PENITENT: Well, up till now, just the opposite has happened!

PRIEST: But these are just moments. And then, tell me, what is earthly life compared with eternity? Isn't it just a moment?

PENITENT: That's so. But it's a moment we have to live through, isn't it?

PRIEST: Have you any children?

PENITENT: No, because unfortunately the misunderstandings between us came up immediately and so—

PRIEST: And how can you have any outside of a regular family?

PENITENT: I could get divorced and marry again.

PRIEST: But the Church will never allow you to do that. You see, divorce would give only a legal covering to a possible new family, but one of no moral value. For the Church and for Jesus, you remain married to your husband because that is the only union sanctified by the Christian sacrament, do you see?

PENITENT: But what am I to do then? I'm only thirty-two! If my marriage failed, it may have been partly my fault and partly my husband's, but above all it was the fault of what had been taught us by the Church—be virginal till married, have no premarital experiences, it's against God's law. And we stupidly followed that advice ending up in this situation. Now what does the Church say to me? "You've made a mistake, children, so now pay for your mistake to the bitter end, no chance of putting things straight." Does that seem fair to you, Father?

PRIEST: But who says that you would now find yourself in a different situation if you had had premarital experience?

PENITENT: No one tells me so. But I do know that I would have had a better chance to know what I was doing before committing myself finally to marriage. Maybe it wouldn't have counted for anything, but maybe it would have. And now I have this doubt.

PRIEST: Listen, child, it's useless for you to engage in these arguments based on ifs and buts. I am giving you the only advice that can be of any use to you. It's obvious that there was a certain amount of misunderstanding between you and your husband due to the fact that you arrived at the conjugal relationship unprepared, especially from the psychological point of view. Now you must do something—organize a holiday, a trip, or whatever you like, with your husband. Do it in a natural way, as if you wished to speak about your future situation, without implications. Then, when you are together, little by little, perhaps you'll thaw out. Be nice, affectionate, and even a bit naughty . . . that is, sensual. Do you understand? Wear a dress that draws attention to your feminity, undress in a natural way but letting him know that you like him to watch you. In short, you'll see that a new atmosphere will be set up between you. You'll both realize that you were immature before and the desire to be together will spring up again.

PENITENT: Father, solutions like that are only found in cheap romance magazines and in operettas. I don't love my husband any more, he doesn't love me any more. I love someone else and he loves someone else. Do you understand? Love's a deep thing that can't be changed by waving a magic wand.

PRIEST: But you had thought that you loved your husband deeply, didn't you, and then—

PENITENT: Yes, and unluckily I made a mistake. This other thing could be a mistake too, but how can I tell? It's certain, though, that as things stand at present, I'm living this relationship with the greatest responsibility and the honest conviction that it's the right one. That's what counts, isn't it?

PRIEST: Well, then, child, what am I to say to you? I certainly can't give absolution to a person who reasons the way you do. In you, there isn't the slightest desire to emerge from the sinful situation in which you find yourself, do you understand? I really don't know what to say to you. I could say to you that I understand you as a man, but as a priest I have to respect the law of God, do you understand?

PENITENT: I understand, Father, thank you.

CHURCH OF SAN LORENZO, TURIN

PRIEST: When did you last confess?

PENITENT: It must be about a year ago.

PRIEST: Ah, and you haven't approached the sacraments in all that time, have you?

PENITENT: No, I haven't.

PRIEST: Is there some special reason, or some crisis you're going through?

PENITENT: Yes.

PRIEST: And how is it that you've decided to come to confession today?

PENITENT: I just wanted to talk about my situation. So many things have changed that perhaps the Church is willing to talk with a person like me who doesn't respect some of its—

PRIEST: But why do you consider yourself outside the Church? Perhaps you would rather discuss the matter at greater length and in more comfort outside the confessional.

PENITENT: No, I'd rather be here. Outside the confessional, I'd be embarrassed.

PRIEST: Well, then, why do you think you're outside the Church?

PENITENT: It's not that I think I'm outside the Church, it's just that I've been told that I am by the last few priests that I've confessed to. You see, I'm separated from my wife, and I'm living with another woman with whom I have a valid relationship.

PRIEST: I see, she lives like a concubine.

PENITENT: But—

PRIEST: Let's drop those terms, shall we, because nowadays they no longer serve. Let's see, then. How long have you been separated?

PENITENT: Three years.

PRIEST: Legally separated?

PENITENT: Yes.

PRIEST: Have you any children?

PENITENT: Yes, one boy who lives with my wife.

PRIEST: Don't you ever get the feeling that you have some responsibility toward your son?

PENITENT: Of course I do. And I realize that if I could offer him a regular family life, he would gain advantages from it. But it's nobody's fault if this possibility doesn't exist. Between me and my wife there's an incomprehension which makes any kind of conjugal living together impossible. All I can do is ensure the best possible situation for our son with responsibility, attention, and affection. Yes, I'm concerned about these things.

PRIEST: Look, you must think of this. Granted that there is absolutely nothing to be done toward bringing you and your wife together again, you can live separated just the same without forming other fixed relationships, can't you? Because it's one thing for your son to have two parents who are separated but live independent lives and can thus devote themselves to him just the same. It's quite another thing if you have the burden of other people to distract you from these obligations isn't it? Without considering that other children, "irregular" ones, might come. What about it then?

PENITENT: All right, these are rather delicate situations, I agree, but everything can be worked out with a certain amount of responsibility. But, Father, what ought I to do? You say we shouldn't have a fixed relationship. Does that mean that it would be preferable, in your view, for us to have little affairs?

PRIEST: There's abstinence too, isn't there? It's a sacrifice, I know, a big sacrifice, but it's not impossible with God's help. We priests are in that condition, but we don't shoot ourselves because of it, do we?

PENITENT: That's different, you have a vocation. I don't have a vocation for chastity. And what's more, I don't see what good it does anyone for me to remain chaste. God? But I believe that God cares only about my living according to my conscience, doesn't He?

PRIEST: Yes, but living according to one's conscience means, in fact, living according to the laws that God has given us. Otherwise, what sense would it make?

PENITENT: I see. Then I must consider myself outside the Church, since I honestly don't feel that I can live like a saint, as you advise me to do, Father.

PRIEST: Not outside the Church, but in a state of sin, do you see? It may always happen that God enlightens you and that you find the strength to reenter into respect for God's will, may it not?

PENITENT: Listen, Father, I want to ask you something but I want you to give me a completely sincere answer. Do you really think that a man who's still young, like me, and doesn't have the vocation to enter a seminary, can live his life without affective and sexual relations?

PRIEST: What I think doesn't count. It's what God wants that counts. I know it's difficult but not impossible. A man can always have sexual relations, can't he? I said that the fixed commitment, the binding tie, is not advisable, that's all.

PENITENT: Perhaps I didn't make myself clear. I wasn't talking about sexual relations as an outlet. That doesn't interest me. I was speaking of sexual relations as the logical completion of a valid affective relationship. I think that people who are separated don't just miss sex, but also the chance of an exchange of affection with another person, do you see? The advice you give me, Father, reduces everything to a bestial outlet. Is that Christian in your opinion? Because, Father, if that's a Christian way to act, then I'm definitely not a Christian.

PRIEST: I said ... I meant that a man can make a mistake every once in a while. In that sense, I spoke about no fixed commitment. If a man does wrong every once in a while God can forgive him, but if he does wrong constantly and deliberately, how can God then be forgiving?

PENITENT: And does that go for the woman too?

PRIEST: Of course, you know that it's different for the woman. There's gossip, and then there's the danger of maternity ... The problem has other dimensions.

PENITENT: I see. As a man, if I give up a fixed relationship, a few mistakes, some distractions, are allowed without causing me to lose the grace of God. Is that it?

PRIEST: I don't know ... that is, a momentary wrongdoing can be canceled by the confessor, just so long as there is the intention of not doing it again or at least the promise to try not to do it again, right?

PENITENT: I can't manage to accept that kind of reasoning. It all seems like hypocrisy to me, a botching together of theories that don't stand up by themselves. Thanks anyway, Father.

PRIEST: Do you want absolution?

PENITENT: I don't know Father, it's up to you. I still think that a separated man is more honest toward himself and others if he tries to reconstruct a valid relationship rather than having casual affairs every once in a while. And since I already have a relationship, I won't give it up.

PRIEST: Think well before making decisions that take you far from God.

PENITENT: I've thought it over already. I can't abandon a valid solution for . . . for what? You don't offer me any intelligent reason that justifies the thing you ask me to do. Do you understand?

PRIEST: I don't ask you to do anything. I've already told you that it's God who has established these laws.

PENITENT: No. It's the Church that has interpreted the words of God in a certain way. After all, the Church has recently taken back dozens of interpretations of the word of God that were just making people smile. Sooner or later, it will have to alter this one too. Because in these days it doesn't make sense, there's no reason for it any more.

PRIEST: If you have such ideas, I'm certainly not the one who can make you change them. On the other hand, I most certainly can't give you absolution. You understand me, don't you?

PENITENT: In fact, I never asked you for absolution.

PRIEST: All right.

PENITENT: Thanks, Father.


CHURCH OF GESU BUON PASTORE, ROME

PRIEST: How long is it since you confessed?

PENITENT: Father, it's been some time. This is the problem —I'm separated from my husband and now that there's divorce, I feel a bit better, let's say.

PRIEST: You want to be divorced as well?

PENITENT: Well, yes, I think so. Because, after all, it's over four years since we separated and I don't think it's right to stay this way without the possibility of starting life afresh, as it were.

PRIEST: The possibility? The Church doesn't allow such a thing.

PENITENT: But it does allow me to remain a grass widow, as it were, for the rest of my life?

PRIEST: Certainly once you're married, you're bound together for always. Your marriage was a sacrament.

PENITENT: A sacrament—

PRIEST: You were married in church, weren't you?

PENITENT: Certainly we were married in church.

PRIEST: You had every good intention of forming a family?

PENITENT: Well, yes, at the beginning. But then the marriage went wrong.

PRIEST: It must have been partly the fault of one and partly the fault of the other, wasn't it?

PENITENT: Yes.

PRIEST: Well, there may be all sorts of reasons that accompany these difficulties. But the Church doesn't permit you to marry another time.

PENITENT: But, Father, does it seem just or human that I should be left like this?

PRIEST: I don't know, that's quite another question. But I must tell you that the Church doesn't allow a person who has already been married to marry again so long as his or her partner is alive.

PENITENT: So if I vote in favor of a referendum to abolish the divorce law, is it a sin?

PRIEST: As far as I'm concerned, it is. You as a good Christian must recognize the obligation that the believer has to obey God's teachings.

PENITENT: Yes, but ... I can't limit the freedom of other non-Catholics who, married civilly, can start a new life thanks to divorce.

PRIEST: But, you see, that's quite another question. For us Catholics who have been married in church no concession can be made, because our marriage is a sacrament. I'm sorry about your situation, poor woman, I know you suffer, and you know very well how much you've suffered, and how much suffering—

PENITENT: Well, then, I could have relations with a man without getting married.

PRIEST: That would be a sin.

PENITENT: All right, it would be a sin. So I'm fated to stay this way.

PRIEST: Yes.

PENITENT: But I don't think it's fair, it's not human.

PRIEST: Look, one has to decide what point of view one starts out from in order to say, "It's human or not human, Christian or not Christian."

PENITENT: Yes, but I'm just a woman, with—

PRIEST: —with all your special characteristics, of wanting to be loved, of wanting to give a little love, of wanting to create a family. And you've tried, even if I don't know why it went wrong. Anyway, you say you're separated. This separation can be accepted by the Church, but not divorce.

PENITENT: But with separation there's the obligation to be faithful . . . faithful to a ghost.

PRIEST: Yes, exactly.

PENITENT: So if I have relations with another man I'm committing a sin.

PRIEST: If you have a relation with others, you are always sinning, definitely. One cannot be a Christian and have relations with others, do you see?

PENITENT: And so, if I get sick through being "faithful" that's quite all right for the Church.

PRIEST: But, you see, no one forbids all those functions that are natural to you, eh?

PENITENT: All right. Then I must go with a man, mustn't I?

PRIEST: Why?

PENITENT: Oh, goodness, you grant that certain natural functions must take place!

PRIEST: No.

PENITENT: Why not?

PRIEST: It's not necessary. If the body, for example, needs to free itself of certain substances, it frees itself on its own, there is no need to go with another.

PENITENT: Well, then, excuse me, I haven't understood. I mustn't go with another person, but I must satisfy myself on my own? I don't understand.

PRIEST: Not satisfy yourself alone. I didn't mean to say that you should do that. But if the body has substances it doesn't need or if it finds itself, I don't know . . . in a condition like that, it frees itself.

PENITENT: But no, it's not true, Father, it's not true. [*Laughs*]

PRIEST: Well, then apparently all women—

PENITENT: All right then. One has to mortify oneself continually, then, and stay—

PRIEST: I do agree, eh, that a woman may need to go with a man at times. That she feels attracted, that she feels the desire to be together with another person. I can grant that, certainly, but this will never be permitted. It's permitted only in marriage.

PENITENT: Then I have to stay this way all my life, as if I'd taken a vow of chastity, something I certainly haven't done.

PRIEST: All right, you're completely free to do it or not do it. I don't understand your problem, madam. You say you feel the desire to love a man, to be with him. A person can feel this desire, but if she's in the grace of God, she can overcome this desire.

PENITENT: One would have to be heroic, but we're not required to be heroes.

PRIEST: You certainly won't be able to do it alone if you don't pray to Our Lord.

PENITENT: All right. I . . . I'll try, but I don't know, I'm in a state—

PRIEST: Excuse me, but how have things been going in these last months?

PENITENT: Oh, well, so-so.

PRIEST: Have you been good, or have you found—

PENITENT: That's just it, I've found a man.

PRIEST: Always the same one or different ones?

PENITENT: Yes, always the same one.

PRIEST: Is he married too?

PENITENT: No.

PRIEST: And do you meet often?

PENITENT: Well . . .

PRIEST: Once a month?

PENITENT: Once a week, let's say.

PRIEST: And this has made you happy?

PENITENT: Well, of course. Now the problem is . . . well . . . I hoped to be able to straighten out the situation.

PRIEST: By divorce.

PENITENT: Certainly. I would like to marry again.

PRIEST: Certainly not in church. When a person is already married, she cannot come back into church to marry again if her husband is still alive. She must do her best to remain purely and chastely in the condition she's in.

PENITENT: But if I get married civilly after getting divorced, can't I approach the sacraments any more?

PRIEST: Ah, it's unlikely that they'll give you the possibility of approaching the sacraments.

PENITENT: But I can go to church?

PRIEST: Maybe, yes. Always supposing that they don't chase you out again. The Catholics who are married in church can't get divorced, you see. Even if you get a divorce and get married again civilly, your union will be sinful.

PENITENT: Before God?

PRIEST: Before God and the Church.

PENITENT: I see. All right.

PRIEST: Try to pray a little, to be good. Do you always to go mass?

PENITENT: Yes.

PRIEST: With whom do you live now?

PENITENT: I'm alone.

PRIEST: Do you go to work?

PENITENT: Yes, of course.

PRIEST: And do you feel that you work with sufficient diligence and commitment?

PENITENT: Well, yes, I think so. It's work that interests me.

PRIEST: And then, do **you** have some amusements that aren't normal, permissible?

PENITENT: In what sense?

PRIEST: Some shows—

PENITENT: No, whatever happens to be showing.

PRIEST: Do you read indecent books?

PENITENT: No, not especially.

PRIEST: Do you read any good Christian educational books?

PENITENT: I read very little.

PRIEST: Do you feel that you get on well with your workmates and your friends?

PENITENT: I think so. I like being together with other people, very much.

PRIEST: Bad words?

PENITENT: No.[*Laughs*]

PRIEST: Blasphemy?

PENITENT: No.

PRIEST: Do you say a few prayers, morning and evening?

PENITENT: Not many, to tell the truth. I make the sign of the cross.

PRIEST: And the sacraments? For example, your Easter duties?

PENITENT: No, just because of the situation I told you about.

PRIEST: But, listen, how did you happen to come today?

PENITENT: Oh, just like that.

PRIEST: Do you find it difficult to say what you feel? Is that why you don't go to confession?

PENITENT: Mainly that, yes.

PRIEST: Are you glad that you came?

PENITENT: Yes, but I've still got my problems and now you've created others for me.

PRIEST: You see, that's why you must pray more. Pray to receive some good advice to keep yourself in God's grace, to be good, to be pure.

PENITENT: All right. I'll try, but I don't promise anything.

PRIEST: You must promise to behave better, madam. Otherwise, what do you intend doing? Giving up everything?

PENITENT: I don't know.

PRIEST: To find a person who loves you and to set up a family with him. That's what you want, isn't it?

PENITENT: Well, I think it's normal, don't you?

PRIEST: It could be for another person, for a person who isn't married.

PENITENT: Well, all right, but you understand that—

PRIEST: But for someone like you, who is already married and who, unfortunately, is separated from her husband . . .

PENITENT: In short, I'm a kind of "banned" person?

PRIEST: Not yet. If you get married you will be banned by the Church. Naturally, as long as you're in the grace of God, try to pray to Him to help you find the best solution.

PENITENT: All right.

PRIEST: May omnipotent God have mercy on you, forgive your sins, lead you to eternal life. I, by the authority of Our Lord Jesus Christ absolve you of your sins, in the name of the Father, the Son, and the Holy Ghost.

CHURCH OF SAN MICHELE ARCANGELO, PALERMO

PRIEST: Have you any grave sins to confess?

PENITENT: No. That is, I'm in a special situation and I'd like to have your advice about it, Father.

PRIEST: Tell me about it.

PENITENT: I'm married and have been separated from my huband for over four years. He admitted the separation was his fault. Recently, I met a man I've become very fond of and with whom I have a valid relationship now. Since it's my intention to start a new family with him—

PRIEST: How old are you?

PENITENT: Thirty-one.

PRIEST: Have you any children?

PENITENT: No.

PRIEST: Why not?

PENITENT: I don't know. My husband didn't want any.

PRIEST: And how did he manage not to have any?

PENITENT: He was careful.

PRIEST: Let's call a spade a spade—he pulled it out of you before he came?

PENITENT: Well . . . yes.

PRIEST: And so you're separated?

PENITENT: I told you that.

PRIEST: Serves you right! You know you began a marriage in sin and now it's all finished. To avoid having children in that way is a very grave sin. Then you come to the priest and you whine, "Now what shall I do? Now I want another family because I can't do without that thing between the legs." Isn't that it?

PENITENT: Certainly not. Your way of looking at things, Father, is very superficial and, I think, not at all charitable.

PRIEST: Ah, yes, well you can clear out now if you don't like plain speaking. What did you think I'd say to you? "Good girl, you've done very well to do that, do it again, another time, with another man. Go ahead, after all, I'm here to put things right." Did you expect me to say these things to you?

PENITENT: No, of course not. I did expect, though, that before expressing such odious views, you'd try to find out more about the problem. Instead, you're so sure of yourself that you've already judged me without knowing anything at all about me, about my situation, about anything, in fact. So, I thank you and I'll take your advice, I'll clear out.

PRIEST: But, excuse me, you've already told me your little tale. You're separated from your husband, with whom you've sinned right from the start of the marriage. Now you want to go with another. What more do you want to tell me?

PENITENT: Well, there are a lot of things that one could say. It was my husband who didn't want children, and one of the reasons our marriage broke up was that I opposed him. Then, it was he who was more womanly than me. Indeed, the fact that I want to start another family with a man who's wiser and more honest than my husband is due to my desire to live a normal life with normal and valid affection, do you understand?

PRIEST: Sure, I understand everything. But, tell me, who was it that married that monster, your husband? You or me? Who was it who chose him? You or me? Weren't you engaged beforehand? What did you do during your engagement?

PENITENT: Father, let's not go into that. During the engagement period I saw my future husband only about ten times in all. And since I expressed a wish to get to know him better, to be closer to him, my father had my confessor speak to me. The confessor said it was a sin to be too close to a man before marriage. He said that I could only speak to him a bit, that I must not let him take liberties, and the only thing I could permit without falling into sin was a kiss on the forehead. And now, you reproach me for not having done something quite different!

PRIEST: Who was the idiot who told you those things?

PENITENT: The priest who was my confessor at that time.

PRIEST: Well, let's leave it. Let's see, rather, what the present situation is. Have you already been to bed with this new man? Or is it just a question of a liking, as it were—

PENITENT: Yes, I have.

PRIEST: Ah!

PENITENT: Yes.

PRIEST: You didn't waste any time, did you?

PENITENT: Father, I hadn't had any sexual relations for four years.

PRIEST: And you wanted to, eh?

PENITENT: Well, I did miss it, yes.

PRIEST: So you got yourself stuffed real good, did you? How often did he give it to you the first time?

PENITENT: You embarrass me. I don't know.

PRIEST: You didn't count, then?

PENITENT: No.

PRIEST: Well, let's leave it at that. You must remember only one thing. The Church will never—never, I say—permit you to continue along this road. Understand? If you want to form a new family, you must be ready to renounce that grace of God and become a daughter of the devil. Only on this condition, that of damning yourself forever, can you continue along the unhappy road you've started out on.

PENITENT: What ought I to do then, Father? I'm only thirty-one.

PRIEST: It's nobody's fault if things went wrong for you. It's not yours, mine, and certainly not God's. If anything, blame that idiot who advised you not to even look at your fiancé before getting married. All I can say to you is that in a case like this, the Church offers no way out. Either you behave like a good woman who represses her instincts—because they're very strong, eh, by the look of things—or you fall into sin. And I can't do anything at all about it. I can feel compassion for you, that's all. But what use is that?

PENITENT: And if I ask for a divorce?

PRIEST: I was expecting that! Worse than ever. For the Church divorce is as if it had never happened. Do you understand? Don't even think about it. I've already told you what the only solution is.

PENITENT: All right, Father.

PRIEST: Don't be angry with me or with the Church. I know,

your situation is a difficult one. Pray to God and ask Him to tell you how to behave, do you understand?

PENITENT: All right, Father, thanks.

PRIEST: You're welcome, you're welcome.


SAN LORENZO ABBEY, TRENT

PRIEST: May Jesus Christ be praised.

PENITENT: May He always be praised. It's a year since I confessed. I'm separated from my husband and I'm living with another man.

PRIEST: Ah! And this man behaves like a husband?

PENITENT: Yes, of course.

PRIEST: And how often does this, let's say, this relation, take place?

PENITENT: We live together, so—

PRIEST: How many times a week?

PENITENT: How many? I don't know, almost every day.

PRIEST: Other sins?

PENITENT: No, I don't remember.

PRIEST: Do you go to mass every Sunday?

PENITENT: Yes, I go to mass.

PRIEST: Always?

PENITENT: I may have missed a few times, but usually I go.

PRIEST: Do you say your prayers morning and evening?

PENITENT: Yes. But I feel, in view of this situation . . . Do you think that we—

PRIEST: If you want me to give you absolution, you must give up this life, because if you're separated from your husband, why do you have to go live with another man? This is not Christian. If you want to make your Easter duties, you really must leave him.

PENITENT: But it isn't possible!

PRIEST: Well, then, don't imagine I can give you absolution. I can't. I can't because that wouldn't help anyone, it wouldn't count for anything. It would be a sacrilegious confession because, you see, you're in a position which cannot . . . that is not Christian.

PENITENT: But we're not doing anyone any harm, are we?

PRIEST: You are doing harm to yourself.

PENITENT: In what way?

PRIEST: You're both in a state of mortal sin.

PENITENT: But the Church doesn't admit divorce, so there's no possibility of—

PRIEST: Agreed, but you have the possibility of breaking it up. A form of divorce permitted by the Church will never come. Jesus said—

PENITENT: Yes, all right, but I don't believe that Jesus wanted unnatural things—

PRIEST: It's a ruling which is right. One sees that it's right because God doesn't do things that are wrong.

PENITENT: Anyway, if my husband and I have separated it means it was no longer possible to live together, doesn't it? And so, if I made a mistake, isn't there any way of going back?

PRIEST: What was the reason for the separation?

PENITENT: Well, we didn't get on, in any way at all.

PRIEST: There can be a separation, but no remarrying with someone else. Do you understand?

PENITENT: I'm sorry, I don't.

PRIEST: If you want to do that, go ahead. You may say to me, "Who keeps you from giving me absolution?" But it's not I who deny it to you. The fact is that it's not Christian, it's not Christian!

PENITENT: And yet, another time when I confessed, another priest did absolve me.

PRIEST: I know, madam, but probably you didn't explain to him—

PENITENT: Yes I did. He said to me, "The Lord sees all and knows our feelings."

PRIEST: Look, I don't know what that priest thought, but I

really don't feel I can give absolution. You see, you're both in a state of sin. You're married and living with another man. Your marriage hasn't been dissolved, you've dissolved it yourselves.

PENITENT: Dissolved? What do you mean? Dissolved by the Holy Rota, you mean?

PRIEST: No. Look, it isn't that the Holy Rota dissolves marriages, at the most it declares marriages invalid—when they haven't been celebrated in a valid way, let's say.

PENITENT: Yes, all right, but everyone can find pretexts for saying that.

PRIEST: Oh, but the Holy Rota doesn't dissolve marriages on pretexts. It moves very cautiously indeed. If the marriage is valid, the Church cannot dissolve it. It's very obvious that you can live apart from—

PENITENT: Yes, I can live apart. But if I live with another man, I'm a sinner.

PRIEST: Of course.

PENITENT: Oh, very well, but is it possible that the Church—

PRIEST: The Church cannot dissolve a sacrament. "Whom God has joined, let not man put asunder," Jesus said.

PENITENT: Do we have to pay for this mistake for the rest of our lives?

PRIEST: First of all, you should have thought about that before making the mistake. After all, you didn't make up your minds in five minutes!

PENITENT: I know, but it happened partly because, during our engagement, we never—I mean, we barely knew each other. You priests always tell us there mustn't be any sexual relations between engaged persons and so we weren't able to realize we were incompatible earlier on. If we'd been able to check this beforehand—

PRIEST: But why? Can't one check on this by means of normal relations?

PENITENT: Well, I mean relations of a sexual kind, not normal relations. Those are important in marriage, too. Now that a

mistake has been made, you say to me, "I won't give you absolution, because you should have thought about all this
beforehand." That's adding insult to injury.

PRIEST: That's not true. It's you who prevent me from giving
absolution. I can't give absolution to a person who's living in sin
in God's eyes.

PENITENT: I see.

PRIEST: I *can't* give it to you, it's not that I don't *want* to.
Until you cease to live in a state of sin, I can't tell you to ask
God's forgiveness.

PENITENT: But I can draw near to God just the same, can't I?

PRIEST: You can continue to do as you did before.

PENITENT: In other words, this present relationship has
nothing to do with the fact that I can draw near to God.

PRIEST: How's that, has nothing to do with it? It does have
something to do with it. Because if you're in a state of mortal sin,
you can't draw near to God until you have removed this sin.

PENITENT: What does that mean, that I'm in mortal sin?

PRIEST: You're married, and a married woman must live with
her husband and not with another man.

PENITENT: But don't you understand that that's unnatural,
inhuman?

PRIEST: You say that . . . But I can't give you absolution.

PENITENT: All right.

PRIEST: I cannot. After all, who's stopping you from breaking
off this relationship? You're the one who wants to continue living
this way. You wish to go on living with this man and thus to
continue in sin.

PENITENT: Won't I ever be able to draw near to God?

PRIEST: Until such time as you stop living together.

PENITENT: All right, when I decide to separate from him . . .
The only thing is—

PRIEST: —to separate from each other.

PENITENT: So God rejects me.

PRIEST: It's not God who rejects you, but you who force God not to give you—

PENITENT: But I don't believe that, because God is infinite goodness. He can't condemn a person for life because of a mistake they've made, especially when they're not hurting anyone.

PRIEST: You're hurting yourself.

PENITENT: Myself? But in what way?

PRIEST: And the man.

PENITENT: I wouldn't say that. Why?

PRIEST: Spiritual, moral harm, not material harm.

PENITENT: I wouldn't say that. In fact, we're two balanced people, just because—

PRIEST: Yes, yes, you're living like husband and wife!

PENITENT: Exactly.

PRIEST: And this, to you, is nothing? Is this a natural thing?

PENITENT: But we're human beings, we're weak.

PRIEST: Weakness doesn't justify the fact of living in sin. And wanting to go on doing so. You have no intention of separating from this man, do you?

PENITENT: No.

PRIEST: Well, then, I can't . . . You're the one who keeps me from giving absolution.

PENITENT: All right.

PRIEST: Pray to Our Lord to help you arrive at the decision to return to God, to live according to the law of God. Because we must not expect God to do what we want. We're the ones who must do what God wants, as God commands.

PENITENT: All right.

PRIEST: If you don't decide to separate from this man, I can't give you absolution. However, there's still time before Easter, so think about it. Think about it, and trust in God's mercy.

*The following are the most interesting extracts from conversations with priests who are uncompromising.*

CHURCH OF SAN MARCO, VENICE

PRIEST: How long have you been separated from your wife?

PENITENT: For over two years.

PRIEST: Have you any children?

PENITENT: One boy who lives with my parents. I'm very much attached to him.

PRIEST: Did you already have this relationship before you were separated?

PENITENT: No, why?

PRIEST: Don't you understand? I wanted to know whether it was the cause of the separation.

PENITENT: No, no. The fact is that after a marriage has failed, a person can't stay alone. He feels the lack of affection, of a woman who understands him.

PRIEST: Yes, yes, and who warms the bed for him. Go ahead and say it!

PENITENT: It seems somewhat cheap, to me, to reduce the whole thing to a sexual matter.

PRIEST: Leave it to the man who represents God to decide what's cheap and what isn't, see? Don't you go to bed with this, let's say, this companion of yours?

PENITENT: We have a complete relationship, and therefore it is sexual among other things. It's only because of a mistaken upbringing, thanks to the attitude of the Church, that sex is associated with the idea of sin.

PRIEST: You call it a complete relationship, but I would call it a bestial relationship because it's outside every moral law and in hatred of God.

PENITENT: In hatred of God? We love each other even if it is outside of marriage. I refuse to believe that it's an act of hatred toward God.

PRIEST: Well, why have you come here if you already know everything? Confession is a means of obtaining forgiveness for sins, not an expedient for sinning without feeling remorse, as you're trying to make it.

PENITENT: Well, then, what ought I to do? Live alone and in absolute chastity for the rest of my life? Do you think that this is humanly possible? And what for?

PRIEST: You have another alternative open to you, that of the true Christian, of one who wishes to remain in the grace of God. Return to your wife, the woman you chose before God and who has given you a child.

PENITENT: But that's impossible. We've already made every possible effort to get along with each other, but we couldn't. To try to continue a life together that's already broken up, would be disastrous for both of us.

PRIEST: I'm sorry, but in such a case the true Christian has only one alternative. He must live in chastity, concern himself with the upbringing of his son, and to ask God for the strength not to fall into useless temptation.'

CHURCH OF SAN FREDIANO, FLORENCE

PENITENT: But, Father, if I've decided to have relations with another man, it's because this is important to me, do you understand?

PRIEST: Yes, I see. Well, if you're convinced of this, carry on. But I cannot . . . I must convince you otherwise. After all, conviction is a thing that springs from within ourselves. But at the same time, I cannot say to you that you're doing right and your conscience may be at rest. However, if you feel that this is—

PENITENT: But can you absolve me?

PRIEST: No, I can't. I, personally, can give you as many absolutions as you like, but the fact is that there's a state of uneasiness. Now, if this state of uneasiness is not cleared up first, what does absolution mean?

PENITENT: Mean? I don't understand.

PRIEST: It's not that I don't give you absolution, but it becomes fruitless because you're not capable of receiving it. Do you understand? Because, always remember that for an absolution to be valid . . . Absolution is not some sort of magic thing that attaches itself to the person to whom it is given. When we come to confess ourselves, this means converting ourselves, changing our lives. Now, if the person who comes to confess feels that he or she is not capable of changing his or her life, well, then, what is the absolution worth?

PENITENT: I see.

PRIEST: It's not a question of priests refusing absolution. At times this may seem to be a surly attitude, but if it's denied it's because there is an obvious inability to receive it. Maybe, in God's eyes, you may be better off than I am. I tell you this with great sincerity. But I must have some sort of guarantee of your conversion. And you're the one who must give it. So, you see, viewed in these terms, confession becomes something that is stuck on, and then it has no value, has it?

CHURCH OF SAN CLAUDIO, ROME

PRIEST: All right, then, what have you done?

PENITENT: Well, I don't know what I've done. I've been married for several years and it seems to me that there's no physical accord with my husband any more.

PRIEST: Why? Ah, yes. Is it your husband who doesn't want to?

PENITENT: Neither of us feels like it any more. I don't know what's happened.

PRIEST: But you love each other just the same?

PENITENT: We put up with each other now.

PRIEST: How's that? Surround yourselves with delicacy, after which you'll feel better.

PENITENT: But, look, the fact is that—

PRIEST: Everyone has his or her own character. You must understand each other.

PENITENT: It's not a question of character, it's a question of physical incompatibility.

PRIEST: Physical?

PENITENT: Yes. He feels like it with another woman, but not with me. We tried a kind of experiment, you see. I've been with another man too, and I feel pleasure, but with him this doesn't happen any more. So, at a certain point—

PRIEST: You went with another man?

PENITENT: Yes.

PRIEST: How many times did you do this?

PENITENT: A couple of times.

PRIEST: Ah! But is he married?

PENITENT: Separated.

PRIEST: Was he a relative?

PENITENT: No, no.

PRIEST: Well, don't do it again, do you understand? Because even if you can't manage to do it with your husband any more, that doesn't mean that you can sin with others.

PENITENT: All right, but I'd like to know how to solve this problem. What do you advise me to do then?

PRIEST: Ah, yes, yes, Surround yourselves with niceties.

PENITENT: It's not a question of niceties, it's a question of—

PRIEST: But with these niceties love is born again—love and physical attraction, do you see?

PENITENT: But we've tried everything, Father.

PRIEST: Ah, I understand, because he's also— Does he grumble, perhaps? Eh?

PENITENT: Well, you know, we try to take no notice of each other. The situation's got to a point now—

PRIEST: Surely not. Do you cook his meals for him?

PENITENT: Yes.

PRIEST: Do it nicely.

PENITENT: Why? [*Laughs*] Maybe I should put some poison in his food.

PRIEST: No, no, for heaven's sake. Do it nicely. What on earth are you saying? Cook his lunch and dinner nicely, so that he's pleased with what you give him. Make his bed nicely, keep the room in order. Lots of niceties like that.

PENITENT: I see, all right.

PRIEST: But, don't ever go seek love from ... from sinful sources, do you understand?

## A QUESTION OF CONSCIENCE

*In only twenty-one cases did the priest agree, although after hesitations and reservations of various kinds, to give absolution to the separated partner who has formed or is forming a new relationship and has no intention of breaking it off. The full text, taped, of the most significant of these conversations, is given below.*

CHURCH OF SAN CLAUDIO, ROME

PRIEST: How long is it since you confessed?

PENITENT: About a year.

PRIEST: Why such a long time?

PENITENT: I don't know. Maybe the fact that, since I'm separated from my husband and I'm living with another man, I've always been to church but I've never thought of confessing.

PRIEST: And you're living with this man in a complete and total way?

PENITENT: Yes.

PRIEST: Have you had children?

PRIEST: No.

PENITENT: And is this man married too?

PENITENT: Yes, he's separated from his wife, and has no children either. Anyway, what I wanted to ask you is do I have to consider myself outside the Church or not in this situation?

PRIEST: You're living like husband and wife?

PENITENT: Yes, yes just as if we were—

PRIEST: There is complete contact, intimate relations?

PENITENT: Of course.

PRIEST: Very often?

PENITENT: Well, yes.

PRIEST: How old are you, my child?

PENITENT: Thirty-six.

PRIEST: Children haven't come or have you tried to avoid having them?

PENITENT: To tell the truth, we are trying to avoid them until we can get divorced and marry each other, at any rate.

PRIEST: Are you both seeking divorces?

PENITENT: Yes, but it's very difficult because my husband is abroad and it's not possible to trace him.

PRIEST: Well, of course, your situation isn't legal, we agree on that, don't we? I would like, my child, for there to be a period of abstention in this intimacy, if possible. Then, during that period you could be relieved a little from your situation, do you see? And in the circle in which you live, what effect does your living with this man have? How is it justified?

PENITENT: It's not justified. It's accepted, in the sense that it's our own business, it's not that people—

PRIEST: They know you're presently married?

PENITENT: Some know it, others don't.

PRIEST: Do you cause scandal?

PENITENT: No, I certainly don't think so. What does scandal mean?

PRIEST: You two, there are just the two of you?

PENITENT: Yes, but what does it mean, scandal?

PRIEST: That people can be confronted with a bad, evil example.

PENITENT: No, no. Anyway, all you have to do is to look around you. If a person were to be confronted with a bad example from all the cases we see, we ought to be scandalized all the time.

PRIEST: Yes, exactly. We must try not to accept them from others, but not confront others with them either, right?

PENITENT: But we live well, peacefully. We're happy, we're not harming anyone, don't you understand?

PRIEST: And what kind of religious feelings does he have?

PENITENT: Well, you know what men are like, they're baptized, so they're Catholics.

PRIEST: Do you both go to mass?

PENITENT: Yes, we do go to mass. But that's just what I want to know—if I can come to church, or if I'm considered outside the Church.

PRIEST: Well, my child, you're certainly not in order, we're agreed on that, aren't we? But, anyway, you can go to mass. As for the sacraments, as I was saying, if you feel yourselves to be carried away sexually as well as in other ways, well do it then.

PENITENT: Yes.

PRIEST: Not too much, though.

PENITENT: Well, yes. But this—I mean, the intensity of the sexual relations—does it have something to do with—

PRIEST: You see, if you were living peacefully together like brother and sister, no one could say anything to you.

PENITENT: Which is ridiculous.

PRIEST: It would be difficult. If, on the other hand, this episode were to take place once in a while, well, it would be, let's say, like a blasphemer who has the habit of blaspheming. Every once in a while he slips but tries to pull himself up. However, if it were, as you say, an assiduous, constant habit, then . . . because in confession it's necessary to be able to promise at least something, you see, renunciation, do you understand? Because you also live ... you sleep in the same bed, don't you?

PENITENT: Yes, of course.

PRIEST: Really completely. You are in the continual habit of—

PENITENT: Of course.

PRIEST: Well, was it you who decided to come to confession today? You haven't been here, to me, other times?

PENITENT: No.

PRIEST: You really want to be able to take Communion?

PENITENT: Well, not just now, perhaps, but I would like to be able to, but above all I want to try and understand.

PRIEST: Of course, your situation is irregular, it's like two engaged people who are already together before marriage.

PENITENT: But nearly everyone does it now.

PRIEST: My child, this doesn't mean that what's often done is right. There are plenty of thieves, but this doesn't mean that theft is permitted.

PENITENT: But how are these situations viewed by the Church? Are we still considered to be its children or not?

PRIEST: Of course you're still its children, but there are good and bad children, aren't there? Children who are less obedient, less guided by the Church's laws, but always its children because they have been baptized.

PENITENT: It's not that the Church sends us away, then, it's not that we must no longer feel ourselves to be Catholics.

PRIEST: No, it's that you are not in order with your conscience. You don't have the right to grant each other the luxury of the body because both of you already have your own bonds.

PENITENT: All right, but like that I'm not the mistress of my own body, am I?

PRIEST: No, after marriage you're not any more.

PENITENT: And who is?

PRIEST: Your husband, even though you've left him.

PENITENT: That's so, eh? But it's not fair, is it?

PRIEST: Unfair. But the contract entered into is what it is and it should never be broken, my child.

PENITENT: Well, then, when I get my divorce can I feel at ease? Can I come back in as a good child?

PRIEST: You know the Church doesn't accept divorce, don't you?

PENITENT: Well then, Father, what do you say? This is what I wanted to know. Am I in the Church or not? Am I a Catholic or not?

PRIEST: [*Inaudible*]

PENITENT: Sorry, Father, I can't hear you.

PRIEST: Legally, you're a Catholic. Spiritually, my child, you're breaking the Church's laws because you're living in a way that does not conform with its wish.

PENITENT: But before, you said that if I wanted to take Communion you would have given me absolution.

PRIEST: In the hope that you would promise to renounce, at least for a time, the relations—

PENITENT: But how can I promise when I know that I can't keep—

PRIEST: But maybe you could manage without for a few days.

PENITENT: But what meaning would a few days have?

PRIEST: My child, it would mean a renunciation, a mortification, that makes this act more serious. It would represent a return to a legal situation. After all, by now this painful situation is a bit forced, isn't that so?

PENITENT: All right, thanks, Father.

PRIEST: Do you want absolution?

PENITENT: I don't know, Father. If you think it's all right.

PRIEST: Certainly, my child. Have you missed mass?

PENITENT: Sometimes, yes.

PRIEST: And then, my child, you have had relations only with this man, there haven't been other intimate actions with other persons?

PENITENT: No, no.

PRIEST: Have you, my child, done anything by yourself?

PENITENT: No, seeing that I have a man.

PRIEST: Well, yes.

PENITENT: There's a friend of mine who's going through a crisis, in fact. She would like to come to confession but she hasn't the courage. She's thirty-nine and not married. The doctor practically ordered her to have an affective and sexual relationship, but she doesn't know what to do.

PRIEST: [*Inaudible*]

PENITENT: I didn't understand, Father.

PRIEST: Does she have a relationship, this friend of yours?

PENITENT: No, she doesn't, but she has a physical, or physiological, need or whatever you call it.

PRIEST: She satisfies herself?

PENITENT: Well, yes.

PRIEST: It's easy enough to resolve that sort of thing. You bring her here, if you like . . . If you want to come with her—

PENITENT: But is it less serious to satisfy oneself alone than to have relations with a man?

PRIEST: Oh, yes, yes, it's less grave, although, it's against nature. Your own action is more natural, it's true, but it's graver because you go against a sacrament that you've received, while a person who isn't married doesn't have the same situation, does she? And then, if she's in a situation that's abnormal, let's say psychically abnormal, then one can close an eye in this case, can't one?

PENITENT: I see. I'll tell her.

PRIEST: Yes, yes. If you want to bring her here . . . Look, Saturday I won't be here. I'm leaving on Friday and I'll be away for three days.

PENITENT: Are you the parish priest here?

PRIEST: No, I hear a lot of confessions in this church, and I hear them in that confessional where you were before, and I always say nine-o'clock mass. I won't be here, though, from the twenty-sixth till May first. If you want to bring her here to me this week—

PENITENT: All right, I'll see. Thank you, Father.

PRIEST: For penance, say seven Hail Marys to Our Lady. And now, if you wish, I'll serve Communion to you at once.

PENITENT: Oh, it doesn't matter, Father. I have to go now. I'll take it tomorrow morning.

PRIEST: All right, my child. Come every once in a while. It's much better not to shut yourself off, isn't it, my child?

PENITENT: Yes, thank you, Father.

PRIEST: Now I know about your case. We'll talk about it and see if anything new happens. All right?

PENITENT: Yes, Father.

PRIEST: Good day, my child.


CHURCH OF MARIA VERGINE, PISTOIA

PENITENT: Father, I find myself in a special situation. I'm separated from my husband and I'm living with another man. I don't know whether I'm sinning, but I'm a Catholic and I'd like to be at peace with myself.

PRIEST: Look, this is a serious problem. A person is on hot coals and is trying to convince himself that he's fine. It's a serious problem, isn't it? What's one to do?

PENITENT: You see, I've already told myself all the things that you might say to me. I've already done that, but I arrive at the conclusion that we're two people who love each other and who need each other.

PRIEST: Eh, eh, it's a serious problem, bigger than we are. Eh? Are you legally separated?

PENITENT: Yes.

PRIEST: And is he happy about this situation?

PENITENT: Who? My husband?

PRIEST: Yes.

PENITENT: Well, he accepts it.

PRIEST: In other words, you were both agreed to it.

PENITENT: Yes, yes.

PRIEST: So, then . . . this other man is free?

PENITENT: Yes.

PRIEST: Well, then? What's your problem?

PENITENT: Can I be at peace with my conscience? You know, I'm a Catholic—

PRIEST: Well, then, we're back where we started. It's necessary, when a person's in trouble, for him to be convinced of it.

PENITENT: I don't understand.

PRIEST: Eh, it's something a bit . . . well . . . a person finds himself in trouble, he must place himself where he's not in a position—

PENITENT: I would like to feel I was all right.

PRIEST: Yes. that's the problem. It's a difficult thing, I've already told you so. To burn, and to convince oneself that one isn't burning, that's it.

PENITENT: But, after all, we're not doing anyone any harm.

PRIEST: No, no harm. In fact, it's a question of conscience, I do understand that. How is one going to keep this conscience quiet at a certain time? I apologize for the example, it's a bit . . . isn't it, but fire burns of itself, it's a thing that . . . when a person comes close to it, it burns that person. There's nothing to be done. One has to convince oneself that it doesn't burn. These things are rather difficult. I don't know whether you understand me.

PENITENT: Yes.

PRIEST: You understand me well, because you are the one who has set herself this problem. It's difficult to solve.

PENITENT: I know, but you see—

PRIEST: Our Lord, maybe, thinks differently about it from men. It may be that Our Lord understands better than we men do. We can condemn you. We know the moral law, we have principles, so men can condemn you but it may be that God does not condemn you.

PENITENT: I would like to know—

PRIEST: Is it the judgment of God you fear, or that of man?

PENITENT: I don't care about that of man. I mean that. After all, I'm not doing anybody any harm. It's a natural thing for a man and a woman to love each other and be together.

PRIEST: Yes, yes. Ah, no, there's nothing wrong, let's say, in the intrinsic sense of the relation if it were not that there is a special situation to be resolved.

PENITENT: All right, but the fact that I've made a bad marriage can't prevent me from living a normal life, can it?

PRIEST: No one is preventing you.

PENITENT: But the moral law—

PRIEST: No, no one is preventing you from living a normal life. The question is that a person, when she makes a mistake, can't make anyone else pay for it except herself. One can't get rid of one's own responsibilities by knocking at religion's door.

PENITENT: All right. But if divorce were to be admitted by the Church, for instance, the problem wouldn't exist.

PRIEST: I'm convinced that in the end things would be worse if the Church were to agree to divorce. Some situations would be resolved, but some would be worsened. It wouldn't help at all, because in the future it would become a chain.

PENITENT: All right, but one can't pay for a mistake for the rest of one's life. It's not fair, it's not human.

PRIEST: No, it isn't fair and it isn't human. And the Church, at a certain moment, may arrive at a point where this mistake—if there really is a mistake—can be put right.

PENITENT: All right, but everyone knows all too well how annulments are obtained, unfortunately.

PRIEST: Eh, if there are mental reservations naturally. The Church goes against you by force of circumstances because they don't want to make another mistake. The mistake can be removed.

PENITENT: Well, the mistake is that two people don't get along with each other.

PRIEST: Oh, I meant other mistakes. If in the marriage there's been a defect, something that hasn't been ... not regular, the Church puts these errors right. It wishes to remove them. Many marriages are annulled, not for money or something else, but because there hasn't been a true marriage.

PENITENT: Well, let's leave that. It's a long story and not true at all because just recently an annulment was given to an actress, Elsa Martinelli, who was certainly very much married. So there hadn't been mental reservations or anything else. They even had a daughter!

PRIEST: But why do you want to judge others?

PENITENT: It's not a question of judging others. It's just that I notice that certain people in show business and people with money, have annulments granted to them.

PRIEST: You're mistaken, because you believe it's all false and that they obtain everything because of who they are.

PENITENT: Sure.

PRIEST: You're very sure of all this, aren't you?

PENITENT: Yes, because there are too many cases. Look, I can admit that there must be many cases that one doesn't hear about, the more obscure ones, the real ones—

PRIEST: But, excuse me, do you have proof of what you're saying?

PENITENT: No, I can't have proof of it, that's obvious.

PRIEST: And if you don't have proof, how can you judge people?

PENITENT: Well, all right, but everyone knows it.

PRIEST: No, no, you must be fair to other people if you want other people to be fair toward you.

PENITENT: But, you see, it's so obvious. They're the only ones who ever get annulments.

PRIEST: How unkind of you! You suffer a lot, because you're unkind toward others, as you're proving now.

PENITENT: No, it's not unkindness. It's just what one notices, without having any bad feelings.

PRIEST: Look, it's terrible what you're doing. You judge other people perhaps because of your own unhappiness. We all suffer. When we wish to judge others, we're the first to be judged. Indirectly, but we will be, without a doubt.

PENITENT: No, you don't understand. Since the only way out is annulment, everybody tries that by hook or by crook.

PRIEST: All right, we may even think this, but we can't say that so and so did that, etc.

PENITENT: I know, but you must admit, at least, that it's strange that show-business people have gotten married with procedural errors or other loopholes that are useful when it comes to an annulment. Don't you think so?

PRIEST: Well, they may know about it. I don't want to deny this, but until I have proof that the whole thing is a falsity, that the witnesses are not telling the truth, how can I judge the intentions of these persons? I would just be malicious and nothing more.

PENITENT: Yes, it would be malicious. unfortunately, though, since there are so many cases happening all the time, a person who finds herself in a position like mine is naturally a bit baffled.

PRIEST: Ah, to feel baffled is something else, but it can be a sign of ignorance, too, you see.

PENITENT: Sure, but then the Church should remove certain ideas from the heads of common and ignorant people like me. Maybe it should publish the reasons why it grants certain annulments.

PRIEST: Eh, no. One must have faith. This is an important question.

PENITENT: But the newspapers print the news and give certain details.

PRIEST: But you know that the newspapers have to give publicity to those people, they have to fill up the pages. I read them all, I may say, but I don't take too much notice.

PENITENT: That doesn't alter the fact that certain situations puzzle ordinary people.

PRIEST: Yes, indeed. At times, ignorance takes its toll. Let's deal with our own cases. I think that's enough, isn't it?

PENITENT: Yes, yes, all right. But you see, I, for instance, won't even try to start a cause for annulment.

PRIEST: Obviously you don't have sufficient reasons.

PENITENT: But, you see, I could try to find them if I wanted to carry out a deception. But instead—

PRIEST: Well, then, you're already telling me that your case isn't one of those that are envisaged, since there would be deception.

PENITENT: Exactly. My marriage is regular, I mean.

PRIEST: You did things in the regular manner and so there could be no turning back because you've done things, at least according to what you've told me, in a valid manner. And if it is valid, I don't see what can separate you. Certainly not the Church, because the Church has nothing to do with it. You're the ones who got married, it wasn't the Church that made you do it.

PENITENT: Yes, yes, I know. But it was a mistake.

PRIEST: You did it before God. The priest is only a witness, as it were. How could the Church separate you now? It doesn't have the authority, that's all.

PENITENT: Yes, I know, but—

PRIEST: It's something between you both. It's a contract between you both, you who—

PENITENT: We made a mistake and we have to pay for it, you say.

PRIEST: But, excuse me, who can get you out of this contract? The Church doesn't have any authority in the matter. It's not that it doesn't want to, it's just not able to.

PENITENT: Anyway, Father—

PRIEST: You see, I told you, it's a big thing. How can you convince yourself that a thing is impossible, that fire does not burn? Look, yours isn't the first case. Others have brought up the same issue. Perhaps in a different way. But it certainly isn't the fault of the Church.

PENITENT: But I don't say it's the fault of the Church. I say it's the fault of circumstances.

PRIEST: Eh, I know. I don't see where your difficulty lies, really.

PENITENT: It's that I want to be within the Church, that's it.

PRIEST: But nobody is sending you away from the Church, for heaven's sake.

PENITENT: I know, but, for instance, I don't know whether I can take Communion or not.

PRIEST: Eh, it's a serious problem, a problem of conscience. It's up to you, I certainly wouldn't send you away. Anyway, these things are your own business. You're living with a man publicly. If you were to cause a scandal, always supposing that this were to happen—

PENITENT: What do you mean, cause a scandal?

PRIEST: Cause a scandal, I don't know, if you behave . . . They know very well that you're husband and wife, that you're living together, that you're, let's say, doing as you please. If you take Communion in some place where you're well known, do you see? It might cause perplexity. I don't know if I've made myself clear. In a certain sense, people could be scandalized. If, on the other hand, you take Communion outside the area where you're known, you won't cause scandal.

PENITENT: All right. Then I can take Communion if I go to another church not in my own district.

PRIEST: Well, these are things that are between you and God, after all. You confess and say, "I've committed this, but I don't know." It depends—

PENITENT: Well, can you absolve me? That's what I want to know.

PRIEST: I can absolve you, madam, but it depends on your

ideas, you see. That is, it depends how you see it yourself. If you're truly convinced of being all right before God, how can I deny you absolution?

PENITENT: But I don't feel sinful, even though I'm living with a man who isn't my husband.

PRIEST: You don't feel sinful? Are you sure of that?

PENITENT: Yes, certainly. In fact, I may tell you that I'm happy about the love that binds us together.

PRIEST: And you are both content?

PENITENT: It's not that we're content. I'd say that our situation is normal, serene.

PRIEST: And should I disturb this serenity? No, certainly not. Do you understand me?

PENITENT: Yes, yes, that's what I wanted to know.

PRIEST: Should I disturb this state? No, certainly not. So I take it that Our Lord, as He did in the case of the sinner whose soul He did not wish to disturb, will also do with you. And since I am His minister, I certainly will not be the one to disturb your soul. You see, you have found a confessor who is very easygoing, very forbearing. Because, in line with my own conscience, I feel I should not disturb this balance.

PENITENT: Well, then, can I take Communion?

PRIEST: Well, look, not all priests think as I do, do you understand? Because there's a moral law that forbids this, do you see? I can't be the spokesman, the initiator of a new morality. But I could say to you, "Well, take Communion, madam." But you must remember you've found a confessor who understands you. You could go to another priest who sees things differently. The law is very clear on this, you see that, don't you? All right?

PENITENT: Yes, yes.

PRIEST: What do you want me to say? I can't say more than that.

PENITENT: Yes, I thank you.

PRIEST: So, then, you want to confess?

PENITENT: You ask me the questions.

PRIEST: Questions? I don't know ... do you take Communion?

PENITENT: Normally, yes.

PRIEST: Try to cause as little scandal as possible outside, in view of your situation.

PENITENT: Yes, yes. But we mind our own business.

PRIEST: I see. But I merely said that one must be careful and see to it that the people who see a Catholic man and a Catholic woman together outside the sacrament, don't draw conclusions from improper behavior by them in public. Ask God's forgiveness, therefore, for your sins and pray that he may enlighten you, because only he can give you the strength and the faith necessary to overcome certain states of anxiety. And pray often. I think that that's the best solution. And try to be good with and outside the family and society. This is important.

PENITENT: All right.

PRIEST: Say seven Hail Marys, seven Our Fathers, and seven Glorias. Eh?

PENITENT: Yes.

*We report below some interesting extracts from other conversations that ended with absolution.*

## CHURCH OF THE MADONNA DELLA CROCE, FOGGIA

PRIEST: You see, my son, personally I don't feel that I can condemn you for the fact that you've rebuilt a family with another woman, but the Church will never be able to accept this "irregular" state of yours. For the Church your only legal partner is the one you accepted in front of the priest, do you understand?

PENITENT: I understand. But this woman is now my wife only in name. We haven't even seen each other for three years now!

PRIEST: I know, I know.

PENITENT: I can't live isolated, I can't think, "I'm a man that's finished, dead," just because I made a mistake when I was twenty-three.

PRIEST: I know, I know. Now that you've created other commitments, pray to God to help you.

PENITENT: And am I supposed to leave the woman I now love, with whom I have a valid, complete, honest relationship? Do you feel you can assume the responsibility for saying, "It's right for you to leave her?"

PRIEST: I don't say you should leave her.

PENITENT: All right, but can I consider myself a good Christian just the same? Or do I have to consider myself in a permanent state of sin?

PRIEST: My son, in these cases, the only valid judgment is the one that God can give. He sees inside of you, He knows what you feel, He can judge you according to His infinite goodness. Don't be afraid, continue your relationship with this woman.

PENITENT: But can I take Communion?

PRIEST: Well, yes. But you must be careful. The people that know you, that know about this family situation of yours, mustn't see you confess, take Communion, etc. Do you understand? People are ignorant, and they'll immediately say, "Look there, we who are clean, who live according to Christian rules are put on the same plane as one who is a sinner. It's not right." And immediately they'd be angry with us, poor priests who are doing their best to understand people before judging them.

PENITENT: Thank you, Father.

PRIEST: You understand what I mean? Now I'll give you absolution. For penance recite ten Our Fathers, ten Hail Marys, and ten Glorias to our Lord. Now we'll say the Act of Contrition together.

TRENT CATHEDRAL

PRIEST: But, my son, do you really believe that the Church can accept a false position like yours? When a good Christian is married, he is married for his whole life. Even when you're separated, you remain tied to your wife by the sacrament.

PENITENT: That's just what I wanted to know. I think that if the Church has **laid** down this thing that I feel to be deeply unjust and outside of every human situation, then I don't care about being within the Church any more. I did hope that, with times being changed, the Church would have revised some of her stands that are useless.

PRIEST: It's you who say they're useless, my son, because you're angry, because you find yourself in an especially difficult situation.

PENITENT: No, Father, because apart from the fact that it's a serious thing and there are millions of people in the same situation as me and it's a serious thing in itself not to take this into account—apart from that, I'm not angry, as you say, but fully aware of what I'm doing and saying. Have you a moment to listen to me, Father?

PRIEST: Go ahead.

PENITENT: This is what I think. A man of thirty-five, like me, finds himself in this situation. He's married at the age of twenty-five, and after two years he finds himself with nothing, for a whole series of reasons that we needn't go into now. It's a mistake, obviously. But in human nature a certain margin of error is admitted, isn't it?

PRIEST: That's so.

PENITENT: Right. My wife and I made a mistake, and there is absolutely no chance, because we've tried everything possible, of a reconciliation. So then what?

PRIEST: Go on, go on.

PENITENT: Look, Father, consider my situation. And I say

mine, but it's also that of my wife and of millions of other people. At thirty-five I'm supposed to live shut up within myself, not have any more loving or sexual relations with anybody but go ahead with my head tucked under my arm. Isn't that right?

PRIEST: Well, you see—

PENITENT: According to what you're telling me, Father, the mistake that I made can't be put right except by living like a hero or a martyr, whichever you prefer. But, as you teach me, few men, like myself, are heroes or martyrs and we have no ambition to become so. You say there's another solution. I should live according to my principles, in the relationship I've built up with great effort, but outside the Church. If that's the way things really are, Father, well, then, I'll live outside the Church and I won't feel much regret because a Church that establishes and codifies such ridiculous situations, inhuman and asocial situations, cannot be the right Church.

PRIEST: Listen, my son, what can I say against the things you've told me? Not much from the point of view of God's law because it is what it is, you see, and offers no alternatives. From the human point of view, perhaps I can understand you better. You now have a relationship in which you are able to fulfill yourself, and the very fact that you are here, kneeling in my confessional, proves that you are not a person who takes things lightly, doesn't it? So you just go on living that way then, with responsibility, intelligence, and moderation. Seek God within yourself because, you know, there is no reason why God, who knows everything and is infinite justice, shouldn't understand you, you know.

PENITENT: So now, Father, you're telling me that the position isn't so sinful after all, that I'm not rejected by God.

PRIEST: Exactly. The priest's task is to find out the degree of maturity with which a Catholic makes his decisions. Yes, at the beginning I did my best to make you consider the possibility of reunion with your wife, in view of your loneliness. But now I realize that you have already done everything you can. One realizes that from your sensitivity and your education. What did you study?

PENITENT: I have a degree in law.

PRIEST: Good, good. It means that your decisions are not the results of ignorance, you see. The priest is always concerned about that. Men often leave their wives just to have a change, to find another body with which they can let themselves go, do you see? But that's not the case with you, or at any rate I hope not. So carry on as before and ask God to understand you, to help you, without losing the fine serenity and awareness you have, do you understand? Now, I'll give you absolution. It's a special absolution because I shouldn't, but I'll give it to you just the same. All right?

PENITENT: Thank you very much indeed, Father.

## CONCLUSION: SHOULD THERE BE COMPASSION FOR THE SEPARATED?

For the priest, marriage can be dissolved only by the death of one of the two partners, even though the priests admit that a mistaken marriage cannot be corrected except by living a life of loneliness.

The twenty-nine priests who are more lenient reject the possibility of a new relationship for the separated partner, but they take this stand with a certain feeling of embarrassment. Interestingly, some of them suggest that the penitent look for a way to get the marriage ecclesiastically annulled, which is a solution that is substantially identical with divorce.

Nearly all the priests ask whether the separated person has children, and if they do this becomes the main argument against having another relationship. Not one of them, however, explains what happens to the children in the face of their suggested annulment, which of course makes the children illegitimate, since they were born of a marriage that the Church declares never existed.

# VII

## SKIRTING THE ISSUES

ONE THING seems to be confirmed by the reading of the 636 conversations we've taped: confession is in crisis—a crisis that consists of a definite break between the language of the priest and that of the penitent. There is no correspondence between the two positions: one is static, absolutist; the other has been changed by progress, psychology, evolution of thought.

Modern psychology puts forward problems that are too complicated for the priests who have emerged from seminaries in which they've learned that any disobedience to God's law is a sin. This has made them into purveyors of absolutions or nonabsolutions, in line with a definite set of formulae of moral casuistry. The collaboration between theology and psychology, which is taking place at certain levels, has not yet emerged in the confessional.

The priests are endowed with a limited cultural background, and they are in possession of norms suited to a period of history that no longer exists. The discomfort that springs from this is sometimes turned into a real feeling of inferiority. How often has the tape machine recorded phrases such as: "What am I to say to you?" "What do you expect me to do about it?" "That's what the law is and I can't change it"? And this, naturally, contributes

211

to the crisis in vocation as well. "Nobody wants to be a priest any more," was the brutal admission of Monsignor Ivan Illich, one of the most progressive priests in the Church. In fact, the drop in the number of young men entering seminaries is indicative: from 156,000 in 1967, it has dropped to 115,000 in 1971.

## THE ORIGINS OF CONFESSION

These considerations render legitimate two questions: What are the origins of confession? Are these origins of a divine, an ecclesiastical, or a social nature?

In order to answer these questions, we have to go right back to the Old Testament, where the penitential rites are recorded as one of the most recurrent forms of worship in Israel. Lost wars, epidemics, natural calamities, were in fact followed by forms of collective penitence in which people fasted, put ashes on their heads, dressed in sackcloth to placate God (Yahweh) and beg his forgiveness.

In the New Testament, the preaching of Jesus confirms the value of penitence, and the apostles are invited to announce to all peoples that penitence and the remission of sins are the expression of God's mercy toward men. The parable of the prodigal son is a clear exposition of this theme: merciful God seeks out sinners to offer them forgiveness and eternal salvation, on condition that they express repentance and redeem themselves from sin.

All Catholic historiographers therefore date the origin of the sacrament of penitence from the expressed will of Jesus Christ. Non-Catholic historians, on the other hand, maintain that the sacramental character of penitence did not have its origin in the primitive Church, in view of the fact that this Church considered itself to be the Church of Saints and those who stained themselves with grave sins were, for this reason, thrown out of the community forever. Only at a later period, say these historians, in the face of a growing number of Christian sinners, was this severity progressively reduced.

Ecclesiastical penitence has existed only from the sixth century onward when the Council of Toledo (589 A.D.) recommended that "he who repents of his sins should be suspended, first and foremost, from Communion and submitted to the laying on of hands and then restored to Communion according to the judgment of the priest. Those who fall back into their previous sins will be excommunicated."

Only toward the end of the twelfth century did the Church give a theological approval to the sacrament of confession. In the meantime, there had been a progressive reduction of the nature of the penance to the point where it was reduced to the mere reciting of some reparatory prayers, while the rite took place in church, before the altar, with the priest seated on a chair. In the seventeenth century it was established that confession should take place in private, and it is here that the evolution from *public and canonic penitence* to *private auricular penitence* ends.

## IS MAN A SINNER?

Father Nazareno Fabretti writes: "Until yesterday, sin was more a personal than a social matter, a purely private affair between a man or woman and God. Now, however, young people are beginning to ask: What is meant by *offending* God? How can God be *offended* if he's God, that is, infinite goodness? This reasoning can hide many snares, but it is a sign of the evolution taking place in man's conscience. Today, the trend is toward essentials, and toward a concentration on good rather than on evil, and on what is right rather than on the avoidance of what is not right. The youth of today demand that religious and moral life should not be embalmed in external observances."